Ark of Covenant Prayer

*Path to entering the inner world of
Prayer taught by the Holy Spirit*

Rev. David Lee

WESTBOW
PRESS®
A DIVISION OF THOMAS NELSON
& ZONDERVAN

Scripture taken from the Holy Bible, NEW INTERNATIONAL VERSION®. Copyright © 1973, 1978, 1984, 2011 by Biblica, Inc. All rights reserved worldwide. Used by permission. NEW INTERNATIONAL VERSION® and NIV® are registered trademarks of Biblica, Inc. Use of either trademark for the offering of goods or services requires the prior written consent of Biblica US, Inc.

WestBow Press books may be ordered through booksellers or by contacting:

WestBow Press
A Division of Thomas Nelson & Zondervan
1663 Liberty Drive
Bloomington, IN 47403
www.westbowpress.com
1 (866) 928-1240

Because of the dynamic nature of the Internet, any web addresses or links contained in this book may have changed since publication and may no longer be valid. The views expressed in this work are solely those of the author and do not necessarily reflect the views of the publisher, and the publisher hereby disclaims any responsibility for them.

Any people depicted in stock imagery provided by Thinkstock are models, and such images are being used for illustrative purposes only. Certain stock imagery © Thinkstock.

ISBN: 978-1-5127-4847-5 (sc)
ISBN: 978-1-5127-4848-2 (hc)
ISBN: 978-1-5127-4846-8 (e)

Library of Congress Control Number: 2016912325

Print information available on the last page.

WestBow Press rev. date: 06/13/2017

Contents

Words of Invitation

Nothing was heard just like other days. It felt as if I had failed again. My heart felt heavy and drained of energy. I stood up and proceeded to walk out. There was a sudden sound.

"Do not walk out."

Instinctively, I knew it was the voice of the Holy Spirit. I was alone inside the closet. It had been precisely one month, since I began to pray for the voice of God. The voice had sufficient authority to captivate my heart, and it did not allow any room to ignore or resist its power. I had been praying every single day to hear the voice of God, but the disappointment of walking out of the closet without hearing it was becoming common. Despite these failures, my heart possessed a distinct belief.

These are the two.

1. If I am a child of God, I will definitely hear the voice of the Father.
2. If the Bible is word of God, no matter what, the words will be a reality.

These two truths did not allow me to give up, instead I felt driven to pursue the Voice of God through a persistent prayer. Now I do not want you to think that my prayer lasted all day or even for a couple of hours. There were days when I did not reach 30 minutes of prayer. Some days I forgot it altogether. Regardless, God's grace came upon me with a mighty force. Instead of being overwhelmed or moved, I felt bewildered by hearing the voice of the Holy Spirit.

Not certain that I had recognized the voice of the Holy Spirit, I tried to confirm the voice.

"Holy Spirit, are you talking to me right now?"

The Holy Spirit answered without hesitation.

"I am."

How can these feelings be explained in mere words? I would call it a feeling of "Reverence." There was no exaggerated emotion and screaming of "Holy Spirit!" nor displays of expressing my heart-pounding joy. The moment incorporated all that was pure and holy, and didn't allow worldly filth to take place. I was in reverence. It was a serious, quiet, and deepening hour. A worry of hearing the Holy Spirit today, but not tomorrow, raised a question in my mind.

"Holy Spirit! There are things I want to know. Could you answer me?"

Perhaps, it isn't the most appealing question to ask, especially for its manner of directness. Regardless, the Holy Spirit replied with a warming assurance.

"I will, what would you like to ask?"

I asked him about everything I wanted to know. The first question was concerning my wife, which the Holy Spirit answered in a very specific manner. I also asked about my family, about which the Holy Spirit said, "All of your family members will be saved." I asked about my father in-law and mother-in law, and the reply was, "Your father-in-law has 3 powers. He will be healthier than most people. His words will possess authority.

He will share the gospel. All those who hear of it, will return to God. His hand will be filled with power of healing."

Upon questioning further about my wife, the Holy Spirit spoke, "She will be called by people after 5 years. Prepare for the work. Questions went for hours on end and the Holy Spirit answered all with specific and kind words. After the family-related questions, I asked about the church and the ministry. What ministry should I do, and how can church experience a revival? The Holy Spirit answered with these words, "You will conduct a very special ministry. Through your ministry, the entire world will be kindled with fire within 30 years. Through you, Holy Fire will touch them."

By now, much time had passed, because of the many questions and cramping of my legs, I asked a one final question. I thought that the answer would give me a peace of mind in ending the prayer session.

"Holy Spirit! Will I continue to hear your voice?"

The Holy Spirit replied with an affirmation, that I will continue to hear the voice. With gratitude, I ended the prayer session and walked out of the closet. My wife was right at the door, greeting me. Maybe she was curious about the long prayer session. This is what I said,

"I may have heard the Holy Spirit"

My wife looked straight at me without any doubt, and believed me completely. She said that the words just felt natural to believe.

Conversation with Holy Spirit

Hearing the voice of the Holy Spirit became the key in being able to carry on conversation with the Holy Spirit. Around the time that I was starting to hear the Holy Spirit, I made daily visits to 6 ~ 7 different dry cleaners to do alterations on customer clothes. Since the days of seminary in college, my wife and I were accustomed to doing this type of work. My wife would learn the necessary skills first, then she would teach me.

As soon as I arrived back from the dry cleaners, we would cut out patterns and divide up the clothes according to different categories, from which then alterations would be made. Usually, I took the tasks that involved quick alterations, such as hemming, cuffing and resizing waists etc ... On average, 20 to 30 pieces of clothing were altered in a day. Although on busy days more than 50 pieces would be altered. Other alteration experts visited the dry cleaners once or twice a week. Owners of the dry cleaners were favorable towards us, because of my daily visits. These daily visits involved 3 hours of driving on average.

Driving is enjoyable. Three hours on the road didn't bore me. I enjoyed the time spent, even if it involved driving on the same road. Three years of daily driving can become bothersome but it was good for me. What made it so enjoyable was the quality of time spent on listening to sermons, meditating and giving praises. It was always loud and messy at home because of my three boys. It actually felt less burdensome to be outside. I always enjoyed driving, but since the first day of hearing the voice of the Holy Spirit, the hours spent in the car became more valuable than gold. Nobody interrupted me. Three straight hours of non-stop conversation with the Holy Spirit was amazing. Getting in the car meant calling out to the Holy Spirit.

"I am here, Holy Spirit"

The Holy Spirit would answer back right away.

"My dear David."

Over time, our conversations began to grow deeper. I asked a lot of questions regarding the church and God, people in my life and random people on the streets. The Holy Spirit would answer in a very detailed manner regarding the people's attributes, even if I had not known them. Things began to grow even deeper from that point on.

The Ark of the Covenant Prayer

Prayer of my wife and I changed completely since the day in hearing the voice of the Holy Spirit.

One day, Holy Spirit spoke to me in this way,

"David, enter into the Ark of the Covenant"

This seemed too random and did not make much sense, so I asked,

"Holy Spirit, what does 'Enter into the Ark of the Covenant' mean?"

The Holy Spirit told me that only by entering into the Ark of the Covenant, will I receive Gifts. With this, the Holy Spirit started to explain in detail. The Ark of the Covenant prayer is 'experiencing God's glory' and a 'way to receive God's gifts through prayer'. Through the Ark of the Covenant prayer, one can receive Holy Fire and hear the voice of God.

The Holy Spirit told my wife to enter into the Ark of the Covenant as well, and began to explain in detail. As promised, through the Ark of Covenant prayer, my wife and I received mighty gifts. And through it, every hour of prayer resulted in experiencing God's glory.

God's Spiritual Training

Through the Ark of the Covenant Prayer, the prayers of my wife and I experienced a radical change each day. As soon as we were awake, we prayed. Most of the time, my wife would enter the closet to pray first, but some days I started first.

If my wife was praying, I would enter into an intercession beside my bed. I prayed that, through her prayers, God's glory would manifest itself mightily, yielding stronger gifts. If I was in the closet first, my wife would enter into the intercessory prayer as well. We never committed into doing this, but it was the Holy Spirit who led us to pray for each other.

To our amazement, our energetic kids remained fast asleep during the many months of prayer sessions in the closet. Because it went without a single interruption, we talk of it as a 'miracle'. At that time, our kids were only six, three and one-year old. Because they are all boys, this can't be explained in other words, but we recognized it as 'The Work of the Holy Spirit'. Since the Ark of the Covenant Prayer, my wife began to change dramatically. First, came great tears of repenting. Not only once or twice, but continual days of deep repenting that was accompanied with tears.

She shared many symptoms that started to show since the Ark of the Covenant prayers. Since I was able to discern by the Voice of the Holy Spirit, as a response to her symptoms, she wrote all that the Holy Spirit spoke of concerning her symptoms, in a diary.

For a while, she heard a sound of a running motor from the clothes dryer. This caused an interruption to her prayer. None of the nearby houses, not even our home, had any machine that made a dryer sound. Even with this fact, she kept hearing the noise for many days. The Holy Spirit said that the interrupting noise was from Satan. The Words of the Holy Spirit encouraged my wife to not give up, but to counter Satan by praying without interruption for manybhours, until the noise disappeared. Soon, she was able to overcome the attacks of Satan.

Manifestation of Power

As my wife's prayers became more powerful, my prayer grew in power as well. That day, the prayer session was extraordinary. Without being aware of anything, just like on normal days, I entered the closet and began to pray. I prayed as the Holy Spirit lead in hearing His voice. With a request, I began my prayer.

"Holy Spirit, guide my prayer."

And the Holy Spirit guided my prayer to the Ark of the Covenant in petitions, repentance, praising and speaking in tongues. There are no set sequences in prayer, because at times the Holy Spirit says pray only the Ark of the Covenant prayer. Praying in tongues does not have to be involved. I do not pray in tongues much, because you can pray deeply without tongues. That day, it was the same. I asked for the Holy Spirit's guidance, and was being guided.

How long had it been? Suddenly my body felt as if a mighty flame had surrounded me. It felt so hot that even if I was to fall into an ice cube, no cold would be felt. Actually, it felt like the heat would melt the ice away. My body began to sweat due to the heat, and I felt as if I were floating in midair. I would not have thought that within a mere 5 minutes of prayer, such a mighty flame could enter into me. Since, the day of starting the ministry, I began to realize how mighty the power of the fire was.

The Holy Fire that entered into me showed that it possessed an ability to completely create a new spirit in one's being. The Holy Fire in me possessed power to fire up one's snuffed out gifts. Through the Holy Fire, people repented with tears and forgave those whom they hated.

Through the fire laying on hands, the receivers began to experience a similar gifts of Power. I even began to witness through those I laid my hands on performing greater works than my own. Some began to hear the Voice of God within just a two months or less. Some even saw visions and began to interpret them through the Voice of God.

The Holy Fire began by raising up Intercessors first. There was no rule-book in praying intercession. Intercessors would ask God and hear directly from Him to pray in accordance with His will. Through this came visions and gifts of prophesy.

Until then, I had assumed that God would use gifts depending on an individual's personality. But the Holy fire proved me wrong. It was completely capable of changing a person's inner-most being. One lady lived with her husband for 15 years in a single room. Whenever her husband would reach out to her body, she felt as if Satan was trying to devour her. She became frightened. But as the Holy Fire entered into her, love began to grow in their relationship, that led to spiritual conversations and a deep longing to stay in the same room together.

Young ones prophesying and seeing visions wasn't just a word printed in the Bible. Young ones experienced God's glory through the imparting of Fire, soon passing on the Gift of power through their small hands.

The Holy fire healed sickness. A person in prayer experienced a rare phenomenon of feeling the patient's pain. The Holy Spirit's fire healed the patient's sickness. The patients would end up in tears, repenting of their sins. Wherever the Holy Fire manifested itself, Evil spirits fled and the place was filled with a sufficient grace. This wasn't about only healing sickness or chasing demons out, but it represented the power of completely renewing one's inner being. Hallelujah!

Words Taught by the Holy Spirit

For the first 3 months, the Holy Spirit began to explain in great detail how one can experience the Glory of God and receive the Holy Fire.

You may have been intrigued about the topic of 'Holy fire', at least once. Without curiosity, this effort might be meaningless. This book is not centered on simply passing on the knowledge. Just as the Bible carries the Word of God, the words in this book also contain the Holy Spirit's teachings and God's purpose. I am aware that this book can't be compared to the Bible. The Bible does not contain any error. Whereas the words of this book may be influenced by my thoughts and wisdom. Regardless, the author of this book is the Holy Spirit. It is, because this book contains the teachings of the Holy Spirit.

Anyone who reads the Bible to decide which scriptures are correct and wrong, is foolish. The Bible cannot be judged by a human knowledge. The same concept applies to the words in this book. Holy Fire cannot be gained through knowledge nor does it come naturally. The words in this book point to the ways one can receive Holy Fire with great detail and clarity. "How can someone possess such detailed knowledge?" Some might ask. The Bible already contains a great detail concerning these. The readers simply aren't comprehending what it says.

Experiencing God's glory cannot come about through possessing knowledge. As such, the same can be said about not being able to gain Holy Fire through knowledge. Experiencing bGod and Holy Fire place their central emphasis on living with God. Just as, in order to understand parental love, one must live with their parents. Someone might argue that one can understand parental love even when they are apart. This might apply to cases for a brief period.

If one never sees their parents from birth and never received their love, it will be hard to debate that they understand their parent's love. The same can be said about a couple's relationship. If you don't live together or share your life, how can you understand or proclaim feelings of love?

This book operates as a guide. But even if the words in this book contain a detailed explanation, you must understand that it is you who is to experience the Glory of God. If one does not understand how to respond, it is a wasted effort, even with such a great explanation. Now, all of you have been invited to "God's Spiritual Training." The choice is yours, to be trained or not to be trained. No one can force you into doing this, not even God will want to force you. If you take a step forward, God will help you, but committing to this training will require your will and determination.

If you have failed in reviving a church, commit to this training.

If you are determined to hear the Voice of God, commit to this training.

If there is a desire to heal the sick, prophesy, and deliver a prophetic sermon through the voice of God, commit to this training. God wants you to commit to this training. God has already prepared you to receive Holy Fire through this training. Now, are you ready?

Chapter 1

....

The Secret of the Ark
of the Covenant

1. Secret of the Ark of the Covenant

Have you ever heard about the Ark of the Covenant? How much do you know about the Ark of the Covenant? Where is the Ark of the Covenant located? What is the purpose of the Ark of the covenant? Are you aware that when the Apostle John looked up to heaven, there sat the Ark of the Covenant? Do you know how to enter into it? Do you know the gifts that can be received in the Ark of the Covenant? What does the Ark of the Covenant represent?

You will once again realize the importance of the Ark of the covenant through this book, and you will pray the Ark of the covenant prayer. This prayer will change your life completely.

In order to enter into the Ark of the Covenant prayer, you must pray the Tabernacle prayer. Those who are able to open the doors of the Tabernacle are serving Jesus Christ as their king. Only those who receive Jesus as their God and Life, as master of their life, as one who suffered to rise again for His sake, will be able to open the door of the courtyard. Most of all, the courtyard must be approached with the blood of Jesus sprinkled on you.

The Ark of the Covenant is located at the very end of the courtyard. It is not located in the center. We must go through various procedures to reach the Ark of the Covenant. At the Altar of Burnt Offering ego in flesh is put to death, through repentance at the wash basin, giving petition through the Bread of presence, submitting to the Holy Spirit at the lamp stand, and the burning incense represents Holy Spirit's prayer. With these, the path to heaven opens up and allows the lifting of curtains to the Most Holy Place, —where the Ark of the Covenant is placed.

From the gates of the Courtyard through the altar of Burnt Offering, we come to the wash basin, which represents the washing of sinful flesh. This leads to purity. There is a great need for you to become pure in your flesh. Through the Bread of Presence, Lamp Stand, and burning incense, your soul will become pure. Without purity in flesh and holiness in soul, no one can lift the curtains of the Most Holy Place. If you were to approach the Most Holy Place without these procedures, it would result in death. Anyone who takes God's holiness in a light manner will be put to death.

Remember Aaron's two sons. The two sons used worldly fire as a fire for the Alter of Burnt Offering that God did not command. Fire that was used within the Courtyard was from God. Because they considered this lightly, fire of God broke out in burning to death. (Leviticus 10:1-2)

The Holy Spirit always says to me, "It is purity, holiness, and focus." The same answer was given to the following questions,: "How can I receive power?" and "how can my gifts become powerful?"

Now I want to share the words of the Holy Spirit. I also exerted a lot of effort in maintaining purity and holiness. This is the first step. Your heart may want to rush into things, but without proper procedures, the results may be delayed. First, become pure in your flesh.

The key to purity is considering others better than yourself. Engrave those words on your heart. This is the solution that the Holy Spirit has given me. Often, we consider ourselves to be greater than others, staining us with a lasting sin. Even if others appear to be less than our expectations, still consider them better than yourself. When your heart begins to conform to this attitude, you will finally become a person of purity.

The key to holiness is "the condition of being sufficient in God." David confesses that "The the Lord is my shepherd, I lack nothing." (Psalms 23:1). It can also be translated as "I shall not want." It means, since God is with me, there is no desire for other things.

Habakkuk's description of faith can also serve as the key to Holiness.

"Though the fig tree should not blossom, nor fruit be on the vines, the produce of the olive fail and the fields yield no food, the flock be cut off from the fold and there be no herd in the stalls, yet I will rejoice in the LORD; I will take joy in the God of my salvation." (Habakkuk 3:17-18).

Do not think that prophesying serves as a tool for money or means of gaining fame. Such a person will be sharply rebuked.

"But Peter said to him, '"May your silver perish with you, because you thought you could obtain the gift of God with money!"'"(Acts 8:20).

1) Encounter with God at the Ark of the Covenant

When the lust of flesh and mind of the soul wastes away and the spirit begins to act, you will begin to meet with God there. God has been waiting for your spirit to be stirred. The wait of God was necessary, because God interacts only through the spirit.

That very God is within the Ark of the Covenant. If you are to enter the Ark of the Covenant, you will meet the one residing in it. You will also encounter the mighty glory of God. In that very place, conversation with God will happen, and the Lord will be there as well.

You might be aware of the fact that Moses spoke with God in front of the atonement cover, face to face. This is how Moses describes speaking with God,

"And you shall put the mercy seat on the top of the ark, and in the ark you shall put the testimony that I shall give you. There I will meet with you, and from above the mercy seat, from between the two cherubim that are on the ark of the testimony, I will speak with you about all that I will give you in commandment for the people of Israel." (Exodus 25:21- 22)

Some people argue that one must talk to God while facing the atonement cover, because Moses talked with God face to face there. That person may know a lot about the Bible, but he or she is not well tuned about Heaven.

Moses built the tabernacle as God showed him. This is a lot like Noah building an ark through God's instructions. The tasks of both, Moses building the tabernacle and of Noah constructing the Ark must have been a very difficult process. This is because,

4

no one had built a tabernacle before, or it is possible that no one had known the purpose of an ark. It was only possible because God had shown Noah the actual dimensions and gave specific instructions for building the ark.

"They serve a copy and shadow of the heavenly things. For when Moses was about to erect the tent, he was instructed by God, saying, "See that you make everything according to the pattern that was shown you on the mountain." (Hebrews 8:5)

What God had shown to Moses was the Tabernacle of Heaven. Moses saw everything in the Tabernacle as he was being instructed to build a copy of the Tabernacle on earth. The reason for Moses talking with God, while facing the atonement cover, is that Moses was not able to enter the ark of the Covenant. In reality, the ark of the Covenant's size was what stopped Moses from entering it. The ark of Covenant's length was 2.5 cubits, while the length and height was 1.5 cubits. It was a small box.

"They shall make an ark of acacia wood. Two cubits and a half shall be its length, a cubit and a half its breadth, and a cubit and a half its height." (Exodus 25:10)

One cubit is about a length of an average adult's fingertip to the elbow, —an average of about 17.7 to 19.6 inches. Based on a cubit being twenty inches, we can calculate that the Ark of the Covenant's length to fifty inches, and its width and height are each thirty inches, respectively. I often refer the Ark of the Covenant's size to a small apple box. These sizes are very similar.

Maybe a young child could fit in there, but an average sized adult would not be able to enter it. In other words, nobody was able to enter the Ark of the Covenant. What then does the Holy Spirit mean by saying, "Enter into the Ark of the Covenant"? Can it be assumed that it means to slim down a size in entering through the Ark of the Covenant?

Moses was quite average in size, and he would not have dared to enter it. He knew how important the Ark of the Covenant was. So, he was only able to face toward the atonement cover, which is a cover for the Ark of the Covenant. Therefore, Moses did not meet God inside the Ark of the Covenant but rather in front of the atonement cover. If Moses was able to meet God inside the Ark of the Covenant, he would have entered into it and met with God there.

God told me to "Enter into the Ark of the Covenant." This is like Moses meeting God at the atonement cover. I could not comprehend the words of the Holy Spirit, in "Enter into the Ark of the Covenant" because, I was at the very beginning phase of hearing God's voice and did not have a deep knowledge about the Ark of the Covenant.

I had never heard, not even once, about praying inside the Ark of the Covenant. While the Ark of the Covenant containing three different relics was a basic knowledge to me, meeting with God inside the Ark of the Covenant could not be understood. What could I reply but with a "pardon?" to the Holy Spirit's direction in "Enter into the Ark of the Covenant?"

Since that time, the Holy Spirit began to explain and instruct me in a detailed manner, about the meaning in Ark of the Covenant, and how one could enter into it. At first, with complete obedience to His instruction, I entered the Ark of the Covenant. It took a great deal of effort to enter inside and experience God's glory, but the Holy Spirit told me that God's glory would be experienced only by remaining inside the Ark of the Covenant.

I entered the Ark of the Covenant every day and the Holy Spirit gave specific instructions about how one could experience God's glory. One day the Heavens opened up and clouds began to descend down from the opening. It was told to me that the Clouds represented God's glory. Within a moment, the clouds enveloped me. To my amazement, the pores on my body began to open up and breathe the Cloud. The Holy Spirit spoke as the clouds were over me, "Satan will not be able to influence you when these clouds are over you."

Soon afterwards, a beam of light like a laser, came through the opening of Heaven, striking my chest. At first, I wasn't sure what it was, but the Holy Spirit said "That is the Light of Jesus … Light that heals your sickness." I began to realize that the light was a healing light and it was to be used on the sicknesses of the flesh and soul.

The Holy Spirit continued: "Focus so that the light will concentrate onto your chest." So, I tried to prevent the light from dispersing, and suddenly, the end of the light beam began to turn into fire. It was like zooming sunlight through a magnifying glass that burns paper. Part of my chest began to burn with fire. The Holy Spirit said, "Take the fire and move it to where your sickness is." So I began to move around to all the painful areas. It was surprising to watch the fire respond so quickly to my guidance. The light of the Lord turned into a healing light, which began to work in the areas of my pain.

Since that time, I continued to repeat the process, to burn away my sickness and filth. As a result, my body became very healthy. Not only in terms of physical health, but I became mentally clear, increasing my capability to focus.

The fire that moved about my painful areas, began to spin around me. Then, the Fire began to spin around my whole body. I began to sense that my entire body was inflamed. In that moment, I realized that an impartation of power was happening. This was the Holy Spirit's fire. The Holy Spirit was anointing me and imparting power.

2) Another secret in Ark of the Covenant

Until now, I have explained to you the phenomenon that occurs within the Ark of the Covenant. What will soon be disclosed, surpasses the previous phenomenon. Moses talked with God as if face to face and his face was radiant from God's glory. Moses placed a veil over his face as he walked out from the tent because people were afraid of Moses' face shining in radiance. However, the veil was taken away inside the tent.

Maybe Moses could give clearer answers, but the Holy Spirit did tell me a lot of secrets concerning the Ark of the Covenant. Now, I am going to disclose to you those secrets in detail.

The Ark of the Covenant represents God. Do you recall when the Philistines captured the Ark of the Covenant from the Israelites? It is like being robbed of God's Glory. Even though the Ark of the Covenant isn't a weapon, but rather a simple box, it protected and kept itself intact. When the Philistines moved the Ark of the Covenant to Ashdod, the civilians suffered from devastation and tumors. The Ark of Covenant being moved to Gath, through its own power, put the civilians of that town into a great affliction. In Akron, it brought about the same results to that town. In Beth Shemesh, the people who opened the Ark of the Covenant, caused the death of 50,075 people (While some may state that not 50,000, but only 75 people died, the manuscript in Hebrew states the death of 50,075). It can be clearly seen that the Ark of the Covenant reveals God's Glory on its own.

The point that needs to be made is that the importance of the Ark of the Covenant can't be viewed from spiritual aspects alone. As stated, the Ark of the Covenant was a relic that showed God's power. As Moses received power by being with the Ark of the Covenant, how much more will the fullness of God dwell in those who enter into the Ark of the Covenant?

As the ark of the Covenant represents God, being inside of it feels just like being in God's arms. By entering into the Ark of the Covenant even once, it will produce enough faith to solve worldly troubles and hardships. Praying inside yields the same results like that of Moses praying in front of the Atonement Cover.

We all know that the Most Holy Place could only be approached by a High Priest. Even the High Priest could not enter as he willed, but could only enter on July 10th, the atonement day. However, Moses was called as a special High Priest, allowing him to enter whenever he willed. Therefore, the privilege of entering into the Ark of the Covenant today, can also mean being called as a special High Priest.

3) Entering Past the Cherubs at the Atonement Cover

In order to experience God's Glory inside the Ark of the Covenant, we must pass through the entering place. It is the Atonement Cover. The Atonement Cover sits upon the Ark of the Covenant as a covering. The Atonement Cover is the same size as the Ark of the Covenant: horizontally 2.5 cubits and 1.5 cubits vertically. It is designed with some height, so that the sprinkled blood would not drip down. Also, on both ends of the Atonement Cover sits two Cherubs, which faces down towards the Atonement Cover with its wings spread out, in a reverent worship.

The Ark of the Covenant Prayer

(Step 1) Enter the Most Holy Place through a Prayer inTongues
(Speaking in tongue is the key to opening Heaven)

(Step 2) Meet and talk with the Lord at the Most Holy Place
(Voice and Visions begin to open up)

(Step 3) Sprinkle the Blood of Christ at the Atonement Cover
(Can't pass the Cherubs without the Blood of Christ)

(Step 4) Experience God's Glory at the Ark of the Covenant
(The Ark of Covenant represents God's Glory)

(Step 5) Understand God's character through the three relics
(Three relics are what Heaven is all about)

(Stone Tablet)	(Budded Staff)	(Jar of Manna)
Represents Covenant (Hope)	Represents Faith	Represents Love

The Ark of the Covenant was made of acacia wood covered in Gold, but the Atonement Cover was made of 100% pure Gold. Also, notice that the Cherubs and the Atonement Cover were made as a one single piece. It is surprising that the Ark of the Covenant representing God, was made out of an Acacia Wood. The Most High God would choose such a common and feeble-looking Acacia wood. It foretells of a meeting between God and sinners. God as King, desiring those who confess as sinners in meting the lowly are to be met at the Ark of the Covenant.

The Atonement Cover was made of a pure gold. Pure gold means without a single percent of a non pure material. It couldn't be called "Pure" with even 1% of other material in it. The Atonement Cover represents Jesus Christ. Jesus doesn't even have 1% of sin. That is the why the Atonement Cover is made of pure gold. In order to enter into the Ark of the Covenant, we must enter through the Atonement Cover, and that is why we must again sprinkle Jesus's blood at this place. We must sprinkle well. Without doing so, the Cherubs, guarding the way between the Atonement Cover and the Ark of the Covenant, will not let you pass.

Do you recall what was placed to guard the Garden of Eden after God had kicked Adam and Eve out? Yes, it was a Flaming Sword and a Cherub. The Cherubs are guardians of God, and this is terrifying. No evil can withstand these Angels. They possess a great power. They are the angels to be feared by sinners. The Garden of Eden represents Heaven. Not everyone is able to enter the Heaven, and that is why God guards the Heaven through the Cherubs.

Entering the Ark of the Covenant can actually mean entering Heaven. Heaven can be experienced by entering the Ark of the Covenant, because inside of it contains all 3 aspects of Heaven.

4) Ark of Covenant and Three relics

We are accustomed to knowing 1 Corinthians chapter 13 as the love discourse. I was also taught that way during my spiritual growth. However, as the walk with the Holy Spirit continued on, a new understanding was given to me. It wasn't a Chapter about Love, but rather a discourse about Heaven. If it is spoken of as the Love chapter, then Faith and Hope become somewhat under valued. But how important are faith and hope! Of course, love is the greatest of them all, but so are Faith and Hope. They are both the greatest. It is just that love is the greatest of them all, without undervaluing faith and hope.

The Holy Spirit told me that "faith is what Heaven is all about." With that, I was able to grasp the meaning of Faith. I really like 1 Corinthians chapter 12 and 14. As one who instructs others, especially for Holy Spirit ministries, Chapter 12 and 14 are a crucial part in the book. But there was always an odd feeling to this. "Why is Chapter 13 in between the chapters 12 and 14? The faith that I know, is what Heaven is all about. Why is love the greatest of them all? Wouldn't Hope be of some importance as well?"

Yes, Paul's utterance of "but have not love, I am only a resounding gong or a clanging cymbal" can be applied and understood in such a way. But to end the argument, with just based on the utterance felt at unease. Suddenly, the mystery of the context began to be solved as the relationship between my children and I were placed side by side.

The truth is, my sons receive 'Faith', 'Hope' and 'Love' from me. If a Father promises the son a gift, the son believes that it will happen, receiving it with 'Faith'. The words of his father also create hope. Without wavering in the belief that the Father will keep promise, the son holds onto 'Hope'. Through it all, the child experiences the father's 'Love'.

Within the Ark of the Covenant, there are 3 relics. At the time of Exodus, only the stone tablets were laid inside. That is why, when Solomon dedicated the Temple to God, it was written: "There was nothing in the ark except the two stone tablets ... (1 Kg 8:)." Did Philistines soldiers take the Aaron's budded staff and Jar of Manna? No, it wasn't that. From the very start, Aaron's budded staff and Golden Jar of Manna did not sit inside the Ark of the Covenant. Rather, these were laid in front of the Ark of the Covenant. Why? You are correct. Because, it was not able to fit inside. The size of the Ark was not meant for a staff or a Jar to be placed inside.

Surprisingly, Hebrews 9 states that "This ark contained the gold jar of manna, Aaron's staff that had budded, and the stone tablets of the covenant." Why is this stated differently between the Scriptures? Actually, there is no tension at all. The Ark of the Covenant mentioned by Solomon is of the earthly kind. What the Author of Hebrews mentions is one in the Heaven, the Ark of the Covenant. Apostle John also saw the Heavenly Ark of the Covenant. He states: "Then God's temple in heaven was opened, and within his temple was seen the ark of his covenant ...(Rev 11:19)"

The Ark of the Covenant that we are to enter is not the earthly one, but is of the heavenly one. The heavenly Ark of the Covenant mentioned by the Hebrews author, includes the 3 relics. The 3 relics are no other than "Aaron's Budded Staff," "Jar of Manna," and "Stone Tablets." These 3 relics are the components of Heaven. Heaven is filled with these 3 things.

Heaven is a place of Faith. Aaron's budded staff represents faith. A living bud branching out of dead tree is only possible through faith. The jar of manna is about love. It represents 40 years of continuous providence for the Israelite, and the very same loving God still provides daily bread for his children. The stone tablet represents the Covenant. What was spoken through the Bible became fulfilled without any error, and even to its smallest letter. All scriptures will be fulfilled in the future. God's promising words will allow us to grasp 'hope'. Within the Ark of the Covenant, faith, hope and love are placed. This is about God's attributes. That is why the feeling of being one with God becomes possible inside the Ark of the Covenant.

Faith will become mighty inside the Ark of the Covenant. Hope will grow inside the Ark of the Covenant. Within the Ark of the Covenant, you will learn what love is. All these things happen within the Ark of the Covenant. Through it, we will encounter God. Also, the Lord will meet us inside the Ark of the Covenant. There will be an inexpressible hug with the Lord. Conversations with the Holy Spirit will take place. Hallelujah!

Ark of Covenant Prayer

2. Benefits from the Ark of the Covenant

Many benefits can be gained in the Ark of the Covenant. God made the tabernacle to be the center of the Israelites' lives through Moses. The tabernacle must be in our present lives today. Our body is the temple (1 Corinthians 3:16). Knowing the true benefits of the tabernacle will lead us in living a heavenly life.

1) Representing the blood of Christ

The tabernacle consisted of worshiping 365 days a year. Countless animals were slain. When King Solomon first became a king, he offered up one thousand sacrifices on the high place of Gibeon.

"The king went to Gibeon to offer sacrifices, for that was the most important high place, and Solomon offered a thousand burnt offerings on that altar."(1Kg 3:4)

Burnt offering is given by burning up a sacrifice. One thousand sacrifices represents at least one thousand animals being offered up. Solomon pleased God through these sacrifices and God gave him wisdom, honor and riches.

Solomon's dedication does not end here. When the 7 years of construction on God's temple was done, he held a celebration of temple completion with a great sacrifice.

"Solomon offered a sacrifice of fellowship offerings to the LORD twenty-two thousand cattle and a hundred and twenty thousand sheep and goats. So the king and all the Israelites dedicated the temple of the LORD. On that same day the king consecrated the middle part of the courtyard in front of the temple of the LORD, and there he offered burnt offerings, grain offerings and the fat of the fellowship offerings, because the bronze altar before the LORD was too small to hold the burnt offerings, the grain offerings and the fat of the fellowship offerings. So Solomon observed the festival at that time, and all Israel with him--a vast assembly, people from Lebo Hamath to the Wadi of Egypt. They celebrated it before the LORD our God for seven days and seven days more, fourteen days in all." (1Kg 8:63-65).

The animals offered during the celebration of the temple completion were: 22,000 cows and 120,000 sheep. All together, that amounts to 142,000 animals. The Celebration of the temple completion was held in a duration of 14 days, which means 10,000 cows and sheep were offered on a daily basis.

The Temple of Solomon is smaller in scale than the tabernacle of Moses. The Bible says, "The temple that King Solomon built for the LORD was sixty cubits long, twenty wide and thirty high." (1King 6:2) The temple is quite small for the 7 years of construction, but the Bible plainly states its measurements. By estimating a cubit to 19.7 inches, the temple of Solomon is 1181.1 inches in length, 393.7 in width and 590.5 in height. This is only about 1/4 the size of a soccer field. How much blood would have been spilled by ten thousand animals in this small space?

What could have caused Solomon to offer up the blood of so many animals to God? Did God require this of him, or could it be that God needed to shed great amounts of blood? To know this cause, the 10th plague of Egypt must be understood. God inflicted Ten plagues on Egypt so that the Israelites would be set free to depart the land. The last plague was a death of all the first born. This plague was not only for the Egyptians, but for the Israelites as well. But God showed a way to escape this plague through Moses.

"When the LORD goes through the land to strike down the Egyptians, he will see the blood on the top and sides of the door frame at the homes of the Jews and will pass over that doorway, and he will not permit the destroyer to enter your houses and strike you down." (Ex12:23)

It was told, the plague of death would only pass over those that had smeared a blood of a slain lamb on the door frames. The household with smeared blood did not receive any plague. This blood represents the blood of Christ. Anyone sprinkled with the blood of the Christ will not see death.

"Look, the Lamb of God, who takes away the sin of the world!" (John 1:29)

The Bible speaks of Jesus as "the Lamb of God." Jesus bore our sins and to redeem us, he took up the cross. Therefore, anyone sprinkled with the blood of Jesus will receive redemption.

The Blood spilled at the tabernacle represents the blood poured out from the Lord. The reason sacrifices are given 365 days in a year, is because Jesus still bleeds for the sinners.

2) Must be Holy and Pure

Through the Tabernacle, we become more pure and holy. Animals led to the tabernacle were all slain.

The animals' blood had to be poured out before being placed upon the altar. Each animal must be put to death before becoming a burnt offering. There would be a significant impact in worship, if the animal is not completely dead. The animals must be slain. The dead animals represent the need for the death of our flesh-ego. If our ego is not dead, we will not be able to offer up a true worship.

Hands were laid on the animals that were brought to the Altar of burnt offerings. It was not the priest who laid the hands on the animal, but the person who was offering the animal were to lay the hands on the animal.

"The elders of the community are to lay their hands on the bull's head before the LORD, and the bull shall be slaughtered before the LORD." (Leviticus 4:15)

If the priests had sinned, the priests would lay their hands on the animal. Likewise, if the elders had sinned, the elders would lay on their hands. If a person, who brought the animal, had sinned, that person would personally lay hands on the animal. What does this represent? It means "I will burn like the animal."

The Tabernacle has the wash basin. Priests had to go through the wash basin, in order to enter the holy place. It was to wash off the blood of the animals from their hands and feet.

"Aaron and his sons are to wash their hands and feet with water from it. Whenever they enter the Tent of Meeting, they shall wash with water, so that they will not die. Also, when they approach the altar to minister by presenting an offering made to the LORD by fire," (Exodus 30:19)

Likewise, we must repent daily. By doing so, we will be able to worship in truth that leads to experiencing God's Glory.

3) Experiencing God's Glory

When Moses had finished the tabernacle, the cloud that represents God's glory filled the place.

"Moses could not enter the Tent of Meeting, because the cloud had settled upon it, and the glory of the LORD filled the tabernacle." (Ex 40:35)

The same result came about when Solomon completed the temple. It was filled with the clouds of God's Glory.
"And the priests could not perform their service because of the cloud, for the glory of the LORD filled his temple." (1 Kings 8:11)
All things in the tabernacle existed for God's glory. All the relics were prepared for God's Glory, as well. The Altar of burnt offering and the wash basin is for a preparation in entering the holy place, and only by being transformed into a true worshiper at the holy place, then the worshiper will experience God's Glory.
As repentance takes place at the courtyard, the Holy place is involved with worship. And you will converse deeply with God at the most Holy place.

4) Hearing God's Voice

One of the benefits that can be gained at the Tabernacle is hearing God's voice. Moses conversed with God at the Atonement cover. This cover is located inside the most holy place. The Atonement cover is placed over the Ark of the Covenant. The sprinkling of blood was also performed on the atonement cover. In place of the high priests, blood of cows were sprinkled. And in the place of the people, the blood of lambs were sprinkled. The blood of animals represent the blood of Jesus.

"and he gave four carts and eight oxen to the Merarites, as their work required. They were all under the direction of Ithamar son of Aaron, the priest. But Moses did not give any to the Kohathites, because they were to carry on their shoulders the holy things, for which they were responsible." (Numbers 7:8-9)

3. Structure of the Tabernacle

To help in understanding holiness, the Holy Spirit provided some insight regarding the tabernacle. As the teachings on the tabernacle began, a surpassing grace was poured out on me. Understanding the tabernacle leads to an understanding of the Bible and the kingdom of God. Moses recorded about the construction of the tabernacle with great detail.

"Make the tabernacle with ten curtains of finely twisted linen and blue, purple and scarlet yarn, with cherubim worked into them by a skilled craftsman."(Ex 26:1)

Construction of the tabernacle through Moses was followed in accordance with the instructions given by God. Noah's ark was done in a similar manner. God's instructions about the tabernacle came with a very detailed explanation to Moses, and it was carried out exactly as instructed. And the tabernacle saw its completion.

To derive an experience that is holy, the ritual processes of the tabernacle need to be observed. The ritual of the tabernacle is a very important aspect in relation to our spiritual lives. Without gaining an understanding of the tabernacle ritual, an understanding of holiness, purity and of focusing on God cannot be grasped either.

As mentioned, the tabernacle includes the courtyard and tent of meeting. There are various ritual processes that take place inside the tabernacle. The most distinctive process was concerning an atonement ritual. One can easily notice that all the atonement processes are simply related to 'cleanliness'.

Temple means a place where God dwells. Its origin takes shape as a type of tabernacle, but that was replaced by a temple during the residing period at Canaan. Moses began the construction of the tabernacle through God's initiative. And this tabernacle moved about from a place to place until entering the land of Canaan. Its last stop was at Gilgal.

The route of the tabernacle began with the conquering of the Castle at Jericho, and at several other places until they reached Shiloh. Without the need for more travel, a temple was erected at that location. We will introduce a verse that tells of its transformation from the tabernacle to a temple.

"Once they had finished eating and drinking in Shiloh, Hannah stood up. Now Eli the priest was sitting on a chair by the doorpost of the LORD'S temple." (1 Samuel 1:9)

The tabernacle and the temple are the same. The only difference is that the Tabernacle is used in times of migration; while, the temple in time of settlement. The twelve tribes of Israelites were grouped by centering around the tabernacle in north, east, south and west.

Our knowledge of the tabernacle is due to the detailed writings in the Bible. Isn't it amazing that 50 books (Exodus 13, Leviticus 18, Numbers 13, Deuteronomy 2, Hebrews 4) in the Bible mention the tabernacle? The will of God cannot be understood apart from the tabernacle. God's will can be grasped through the tabernacle. Jesus can be known through the tabernacle, as well as the Holy Spirit. The Bible can be viewed as whole by understanding the tabernacle. The purpose of Leviticus being included as one of the books in the Bible can be revealed through the tabernacle. Leviticus will be completely transformed from its boring image to a whole new book that will earn your eager attention.

1) Tabernacle entrance

The gate of the tabernacle is made of four different twisted linen curtains.

The tabernacle constructed by Moses had its entrance only at the east side. Its length from east to the west was 50 cubits (about 82 feet) and its length from south to the north was 100 cubits (about 328 feet). And the entrance to the tent was made in blue, purple, and scarlet yarn and white, finely twisted linen that represents Jesus.

"For the entrance to the courtyard, provide a curtain twenty cubits long, of blue, purple and scarlet yarn and finely twisted linen--the work of an embroiderer--with four posts and four bases."(Exodus 27:16)

The blue represents Jesus as life. The purple represents Jesus as King. The scarlet represents Jesus having suffered. The white represents the resurrected Jesus.

The gate of the tabernacle is 20 cubit (about 32 feet). It is great in size. Since the eastside wall of the tabernacle stretches 50 cubit (about 82 feet), nearly half the length is gate. Jesus is the gate, a gate that paths to redemption. Without passing through Jesus, redemption cannot be attained. Through Jesus as the gate, God will become approachable.

"I am the gate. Those who come in by me will be saved; they will come in and go out and find pasture." (John 10:9)

Yes, Jesus is the path that leads to God. Only by Jesus, will we be able to approach God. Jesus does not turn-away anyone. The learned and unlearned can both approach God. The wealthy and the poor can also approach God. There is no favoritism towards man or woman, or towards those who are enslaved or free.

The only gate to the tabernacle is located on the east wall, as the sun rises in the east. Jesus came as the light of the world. The light of Jesus will shine on those who approach Jesus. Souls will be revived and diseases will be healed.

"But for you who obey me, my saving power will rise on you like the sun and bring healing like the sun's rays. You will be as free and happy as calves let out of a stall." (Mal 4:2)

2) The Altar of Burnt offering and wash basin

Animals are burned at the altar of burnt offering. Hands were laid upon the animals that were brought to the altar of burnt offering.

"He shall bring the bull to the entrance of the tent, put his hand on its head, and kill it there in the LORD's presence." (Leviticus 4:4)

Do you know what it means to lay hands on the animals that are to be burned up? The laying on of hands creates a physical contact. This is done so that gifts will pass on to another, but it is also performed so that one will be able to transfer all of oneself to another. It means that the passing on of one's sins by laying on of hands is done by the sinner to the animal, because a person cannot be burned up at the altar of burnt offering. In essence, even though it is the animal that is slain at the altar of burnt offering, it is the person that dies through that animal.

Jesus is portrayed as the "Lamb" in the Bible. Jesus has revealed that on his accord, he will become the offering. He means to go on the top of the altar of burnt offerings and be burnt to death like an animal. He means to bear the sins of the sinners.

Romans chapter 6 verse 23 says that the "Wages of sin is death." Sin must be paid in full. The result of paying in full is death. A sinful man must be put to death. But Jesus means to pay off the wages of sin for the sake of the sinners.

The altar of burnt offering represents the baptism of the Holy Spirit. Believing Jesus as the savior, requires the spiritual baptism first, then the baptism of the flesh. The spiritual baptism represents the baptism of the Holy Spirit, whereas baptism of the flesh is represented by the water baptism. This order can be reversed. At times, the flesh can come first. One can receive the water baptism by someone else's initiative. It can be a part of a family tradition. Regardless, the spiritual baptism, that is the baptism of the Holy Spirit, must take place in a person to become saved. The water baptism is not enough to redeem a person. A very crucial step in becoming saved involves the baptism of the Holy Spirit.

Our bodies have already been offered up to God at the Altar of burnt offering. This is the baptism of the Holy Spirit. It must be placed in priority over bodily cleanliness. Therefore, a person receiving the water baptism must first accept Jesus as their savior.

"If you confess that Jesus is Lord and believe that God raised him from death, you will be saved. For it is by our faith that we are put right with God; it is by our confession that we are saved." (Romans 10:9)

The wash basin is a large dish that contains water. The Bible emphasizes through Exodus 30:19-20 that "Aaron and his sons are to use the water to wash their hands and feet before they go into the Tent or approach the altar to offer the food offering. Then they will not be killed." Tent means the Holy Place and the most Holy Place. The wash basin is placed in between the altar of burnt offering and the tent.

The priests conducted the ritual without putting on their shoes. The floor of the temple was a bare earth. Have you lived on the ground without having shoes on? The feet becomes dirty in no time. Is it the ground only? The Altar of burnt offering was a place where the slaughtering of the animals and sprinkling of the blood were conducted. The hands and body of the priests were always covered in the blood of the animals. That is why the instruction on washing of the body was given.

The wash basin represents a water baptism. Our bodies have been cleansed at the wash basin. The water baptism is a symbol of Jesus's burial and resurrection. All of our sins have been forgiven through the water baptism and we have been born again through Christ.

"Therefore, if anyone is in Christ, he is a new creation; the old has gone, the new has come!" (2 Corinthians 5:17)

3) The Holy Place (Bread of the presence, Lamp stand, altar of incense)

The tent is located behind the wash basin within the tabernacle. This tent is divided into the Holy Place and the Most Holy Place.

The Holy Place can only be approached by the priests, where the bread of presence, lamp stand, and altar of incense are placed. The Holy Place is a place of worship. Those who have been sanctified in the courtyard undergo a holy transformation inside the Holy Place. Only the holy people are able to worship. The Holy Place is an environment for worshiping God in spirit and truth. God is looking for those who worship him in truth and spirit, which means those who worship at the Holy Place.

"Yet a time is coming and has now come when the true worshipers will worship the Father in spirit and truth, for they are the kind of worshipers the Father seeks." (John 4:23)

A worshiper becomes true only at the Holy Place. God does not seek the ones remaining at the courtyard. God will seek the true worshipers at the Holy Place. That is why we must always remain at the Holy Place.

Now the relics of the Holy Place will be discussed in detail.

As one enters the Holy Place, the bread of presence is located on the right side. The bread of presence includes 12 loaves that are made early in the day right before the Sabbath, to be brought out on the Sabbath morning. The meaning of the bread of presence resides in Jesus as the bread of life. Jesus said "I am the bread of life" (John 6:48). The Israelites ate manna for 40 years. This manna also represents Jesus. We must eat manna daily. We must also recognize and believe that Jesus is the bread of life. Those who worship at the Holy Place do not partake of worldly bread. People who partake of worldly bread are brood of the Devil. Worshipers of God are the people who live by relying on Jesus alone.

"I am the living bread that came down from heaven. If anyone eats of this bread, he will live forever. This bread is my flesh, which I will give for the life of the world." (John 6:51)

The left area inside of the Holy Place is for the golden lamp stand. This golden lamp stand is composed of seven lamps on a stand that is made out of a pure gold.

The Holy Place can only be seen through the eyes from the light of the golden lamp stand. It is always dark inside the tent because of its four layers of coverings. The first layer is in blue, purple, scarlet, and white linen twisted to a great scale. The second layer was made from strands of a goat hair. The third layer is made of ram skins that are dyed in red. The fourth layer is made from the hides of sea cows.

There are no windows inside the tent. It is an isolated area separated from holes and open spaces. Can you imagine how dark it was inside the four-layered tent? The priests did not experience darkness nor confusion, when carrying out the service, because the golden lamp stand was shining brightly inside the tent.

The golden lamp stand is made out of one pure gold, shaped into an image of apricot flowers. This represents unchanging faith and a devout belief in redemption. Pure gold does not change in nature. Likewise, apricot flowers are the earliest blooms after the winter's passing. Also, the golden lamp stand branches out into seven lamps. 7 is the number of perfection and victory. With a careful observation, the lamp stand can be seen as having three lamps on each side, with one lamp standing taller in the middle. Without the middle stand, it numbers only 6. 6 is the number of humans and of the devil. The imperfect number becomes perfect through Jesus. The Church needs Jesus. Families need Jesus. An individual needs Jesus. That is how perfection is made.

"Remain in me, and I will remain in you. No branch can bear fruit by itself; it must remain in the vine. Neither can you bear fruit unless you remain in me. I am the vine; you are the branches. If a man remains in me and I in him, he will bear much fruit; apart from me you can do nothing." (John 15:4-5)

Lastly, an altar of incense is placed inside the Holy Place. This altar is placed right in front of the most Holy Place. The altar of incense represents the prayers of the saints. Actually, the altar of incense is to be kept burning throughout 365 days of the year. This Holy incense filled the Holy Place. Likewise, David in his hope prayed that his prayer would be like that of incense.

"May my prayer be set before you like incense; may the lifting up of my hands be like the evening sacrifice." (Psalms 141:2)

In the Book of Revelations, it records that the prayers of saints were lifted up to be laid in front of the lamb.

"And when he had taken it, the four living creatures and the twenty-four elders fell down before the Lamb. Each one had a harp and they were holding golden bowls full of incense, which are the prayers of the saints." (Revelations 5:8)

4) The Most Holy Place (Atonement Cover, Ark of the Covenant)

The atonement cover is located inside the Most Holy Place. The Most Holy Place is in the inner-most part of the tent. This speaks for its utmost importance.

This utmost important Most Holy Place consisted only of the Ark of the Covenant. In other words, it is not the Most Holy Place that is important, but the Ark of the Covenant. The Ark of the Covenant is an actual reality of God. Inside the Ark of the Covenant there are three relics. The author of Hebrews records about the relics below:

". ... which had the golden altar of incense and the gold-covered Ark of the Covenant. This Ark contained the gold jar of manna, Aaron's staff that had budded, and the stone tablets of the Covenant." (Hebrews 9:4)

The gold jar of manna, Aaron's staff that had budded, and the stone tablets of the Covenant inside the Ark represent the being of God. The gold jar of manna represents God as life. Aaron's staff that had budded represents God as resurrection. The stone tablets of the Covenant represent God as the Word.

The Ark of the Covenant will be discussed more in detail later on because, the Ark of the Covenant is a relic that helps us to experience and focus on the glory of God.

4. Prayer of the body, the mind and the spirit

1) Body- Mind – Spirit

The Holy Spirit has revealed many surprises during the spiritual training, but the Ark of the Covenant stood out to be special. As previously stated, the blessings in the Ark of the Covenant are great. Despite this fact, many people are still unaware of the Ark of the Covenant. It is because of its lack of interest. If people were to understand the Ark of the Covenant, this world would undergo a great transformation.

We approach God as a one whole being. This means that we must approach him with our body, mind and spirit. We are well aware that a human being is composed of a body, mind and spirit. Some people may entwine the mind and the spirit, calling it a "Soul." Though thoughts may vary, the spirit and the mind are actually different. This is also spoken for when talking about the body.

The Bible describes humans as having three distinct aspects.

"For the word of God is living and active. Sharper than any double-edged sword, it penetrates even to dividing soul and the spirit, joints and marrow; it judges the thoughts and attitudes of the heart." (Hebrews 4:12)

"May God himself, the God of peace, sanctify you through and through. May your whole spirit, soul and the body be kept blameless at the coming of our Lord Jesus Christ." (1 Thessalonians 5:23)

It is commonly known to call the 3 distinct images that make up a being as "Trichotomy." Meanwhile, some use the term "Dichotomy" to describe a being divided into just spirit and body. However, this kind of knowledge is only useful for the theologians or religious scholars. The true importance resides in our walking with God, which has the required components in our body. We have the body, the mind and the spirit, which walks with God and experiences God's glory.

2) Prayer of the body

We are to use all three aspects, the body, the mind and the spirit in relation to God. Simply because we are made of three parts, it is wrong to think that the body is corrupted and vile. Our body is holy and precious because God has created it. While it is easy for the body to commit a sin that will cause corruption and vileness, God still views our created body as beautiful. What parent would see their child's body as a corrupted and vile being?

A hospitalized patient can have a body that is abnormally shaped. At times, a sense of uneasiness can be experienced by laying hands on those areas. And I do repent of it immediately. Though, what surprises me is the parents. They are not hindered by the child's outer appearances. On the contrary, more love is poured out on them than of a normal child. God does the same. Our appearance is of a greater beauty than the flowers. It would be wrong to assume that our body is corrupted and vile.

God wants our praise and worship, and within these praises and worship, prayer remains at the center. God commands us to pray in the body, the mind and the spirit.

Many people ask how I pray. I always keep the three aspects in mind. These aspects are the "prayer of the body," "prayer of the mind," and "prayer of the spirit." The three prayers are lifted up during the session. First, the "prayer of the body" is prayed. Then, the prayer moves onto the "prayer of the mind." Lastly, it is transformed into the "prayer of the spirit."

Prayer of the body is a prayer of repentance. When we repent our sins, we gain purity.

Another aspect in the prayer of the body is requesting the needs of the body. Our body demands a lot of things. Therefore, there are a lot of requests. Most common prayer of the body is concerning what to eat. People are mainly interested in what to eat and drink. Amazingly, even the believers are no different. That is why we are prone to stop at the prayer of the body. We demand so many things and that is why much time is spent in this prayer of the body. Despite the time spent, our prayers are often not answered. It is that God does not want to answer based on the passions of the flesh.

"When you ask, you do not receive, because you ask with wrong motives, that you may spend what you get on your pleasures." (James 4:3)

People may ask diligently, but these prayers end up in the trash bin. Many do not understand why. Many use this verse "You may ask me for anything in my name, and I will do it."(John 14:14), and protest to God. God remains silent in those times. Many become bitter or regretful toward such a reaction from God, and leave the church.

The prayer of the body deals with an important aspect of our lives, but it rarely gets answered. It is because the needs of the flesh are asked with passions of the flesh. People do not possess a correct understanding in not asking with the passions of the flesh. The passion here is referring to a worldly manner. Asking in accordance with God's will is not asking for passions of the flesh. As stated by Apostle John, the worldly things are "the cravings of sinful man, the lust of his eyes and the boasting of what he has and does." (John 2:16) Not receiving, in spite of asking, is due to asking through the worldly passions.

A person who ends a prayer session in a prayer of the body do not even know who we are praying to. That person does not even know what a prayer is. It's as if an entire day was just spent on "spacing out". As "spacing out" requires an object of interaction, that person chose God to "space out". The person in that type of prayer does not notice God, nor does God take notice of him. That type of prayer reflects a bitter, tough and tiresome life. It is because there is no one to help.

3) Prayer of the mind

The prayer of the mind is a prayer of worship and praise. This prayer can praise God, or thank God for his grace. The prayer of the mind is a fruit formed from the prayer of the body. As the prayer of the body is carried out, it eventually arrives at the prayer of the mind. But most of the people leave the prayer room after the prayer of the body. They are leaving, without even having experienced a real prayer. There comes a time, when prayers seem endless and boring, but we know that a conversation involves an exchange of words. It is regrettable that a person will only speak out and then simply leave.

This is not the case for the prayer of the mind. A person praying the prayer of the mind has petitions with thanksgiving.

There is a praise. This type of person expresses a thankfulness for God's remarkable grace. The prayer of the mind always sheds tears. There are tears in the prayer of the body as well, but the tears from prayer of the body are full of regrets, remorse and a bitter cry. While the prayer of the mind is full of joy and tears of grace. These are the key differences.

However, there isn't much benefit in stopping at the prayer of the mind. There is an emotion and swelling of joy, but it is just as though you were attending a revival. Though, there is emotion and joy at a revival too.

It is as if the dead works were changed to live works and the feelings of first love rising again, but in time, these things disappear without a trace. This is the prayer of the mind, but the prayer of the spirit differs from these.

4) Prayer of the spirit

The Prayer of the spirit is offered inside the Most Holy Place. If the prayer of the body is done at the courtyard, and the prayer of the mind is conducted at the Holy Place, the prayer of the spirit is lifted up at the Most Holy Place.

The Prayer of the spirit is prayed through the spirit. Therefore, no words are needed. The prayer of the body is done through the lips, while the prayer of the mind is conducted with the mind. A person praying the prayer of the spirit does not use words. He or she remains in a stilled state. It is because the glory of God is manifested by being still. How easy it would be if the glory could be experienced through mere lips, or if done by the mind and passions. But the prayer of the spirit is about being still.

No efforts are necessary in seeing the glory of God. There are no thoughts processed in trying to benefit from all this. It is about being still. It is about laying down our will and thoughts. Your emotions must be put in order. Is there a feeling of hatred? If so, sorry, but you shouldn't expect to experience the glory of God. Trying to attain the fire by a mere human effort, and in so doing, become famous? Sorry, but the glory of God will not be manifested on such terms. No matter what knowledge, emotion and will we might have, these things should all be restricted to the prayer of the mind. All these attributes belong to the prayer of the mind. The prayer of the spirit does not allow such things. You must empty out all that you are. Perhaps even the effort of trying to empty oneself should all be laid down.

Just by sitting still, in its time the glory of God will be manifested to you, and the manifestation of God's glory will grow deeper and wider. By praying, the fire of the Holy Spirit will be made manifest to you in no time.

5) Prayer of the Spirit in the Old Testament

Records of the prayer of spirit can be found throughout the Bible. The prophets in the times of the Old Testament prayed spiritual prayers. Jesus and his disciples are the ones who prayed the spiritual prayer in times of the New Testament.

Noah is the first person to have prayed spiritual prayer. Of course, Adam may have prayed the very first. But there are no records of Adam since his exile because of sins committed in the Garden of Eden. Adam's 7th descendant, Enoch, lived 365 years and was lifted up to the heavens without seeing death. The Bible states, "Enoch walked with God; then he was no more, because

God took him away." (Genesis 5:24) However, but we cannot determine if Enoch prayed the spiritual prayer.

Adam's 10th descendant, Noah, prayed spiritual prayers. He is known as the builder of Noah's Ark. The Bible says, "Noah was a righteous man, blameless among the people of his time, and he walked with God." (Genesis 6:9) It is told, eight people survived the flood in all, through the Noah's Ark. Noah listened to the voice of God in building the Ark. Noah had not possessed any knowledge about building the Ark. Unlike the current era, he could not even go on the web to search the word "The Ark." It is likely that many others ridiculed Noah for building The Ark in preparation of a supposedly coming flood.

But Noah made a decision to obey the word of God. Honestly, the words of God to Noah are hard to believe. Let's listen to the following words of God. "I am going to bring floodwaters on the earth to destroy all life under the heavens, every creature that has the breath of life in it. Everything on earth will perish." (Genesis 6:17) If it was you, would you have believed God's words?

But Noah did believe God.

"Noah did everything just as God commanded him." (Genesis 6:22)

Noah built the Ark according to God's word and believed that the world would soon flood. He also took all kinds of animals into the Ark as God instructed. And he waited, as stated by God's words. He did everything according to the commands of God.

What an amazing belief and a great obedience. How could such belief and obedience come about? Aren't you curious? It was because Noah prayed the spiritual prayer. Yes, there are no records of such prayers in the Bible. It only states that he was a righteous man and walked with God. Perhaps, some may even say "Pastor ... that is such a random guess." But lift up the prayer of the spirit, and you will come to believe that what I am saying is true.

Through the prayer of the spirit, you can begin to hear the voice of God. By hearing it, God's commands can be confirmed with an assurance and can be felt. The truth in hearing the voice of God accurately, gives birth to a greater faith. Noah is a man just like us. But he had a different degree of certainty than most of us. This type of certainty comes from hearing the Words of God accurately. This is also the result of the prayer of the spirit. This type of outcome happens by lifting up the prayer of spirit.

Take a look at Abraham. He also heard the voice of God and followed the voice of God. There were times when some had not followed the voice of God. The Bible describes his faith in the following way:

"Against all hope, Abraham in hope believed and so became the father of many nations, just as it had been said to him, "So shall your offspring be." Without weakening in his faith, he faced the fact that his the body was as good as dead--since he was about a hundred years old and that Sarah's womb was also dead. Yet he did not waver through unbelief regarding the promise of God, but was strengthened in his faith and gave glory to God, being fully persuaded that God had power to do what he had promised. This is why "it was credited to him as righteousness." (Romans 4:18-22)

Actually, Abraham possessed a great faith because he heard the words of "So shall your offspring be." He was a person who heard the words of God correctly, precisely and accurately. Let us answer honestly. If you were 99 years old like Abraham, and Sarah was 89 years old, would you have believed God who had promised to provide for a child? Probably most of us would have answered "No."

Really, this isn't easy. But Abraham exemplified his faith through God's words. It is a great faith. This kind of faith is only attainable through the prayer of spirit. The prayer of spirit not only brings an assurance, but allows a greater faith.

God in the spirit approached Abraham. Yes, before the destruction of Sodom and Gomorrah, God did appear to Abraham in the appearance of an Angel. But when the words of Abraham's descendants being more than the stars in the heavens and the sands on the shore were spoken, God was with him in spirit.

"Then the word of the LORD came to him : "This man will not be your heir, but a son coming from your own the body will be your heir." He took him outside and said, "Look up at the heavens and count the stars--if indeed you can count them." Then he said to him, "So shall your offspring be" Abraham believed the LORD, and he credited it to him as righteousness. (Genesis 15:4-6)"

As Abraham walked with God in The spirit, so did Moses. Moses conversed with God at the burning bush. Later on, he followed the voice of God in building the tabernacle and conversed with God at the Most Holy Place.

"With him I speak face to face, clearly and not in riddles; he sees the form of the LORD. Why then were you not afraid to speak against my servant Moses?" (Numbers12:8)

The place where Moses went in order to converse with God is the Most Holy Place. The Ark of the Covenant was inside the Most Holy Place. On top of The Ark of the Covenant laid the atonement cover upon which sat two cherubs with their wings wide open to protect The Ark of the Covenant. Moses heard the voice of God at this atonement cover. The Most Holy Place is the most sacred place worshiped in the spirit. This is just like the Holy ground near the burning bush, which no one could approach, but required the removal of sandals before entering. That is why even the high priest could only enter once a year on the day of the atonement. God commanded that no one was to approach the Most Holy Place in a light manner.

Moses, like Jesus, was well acquainted in the prayer of spirit. As we are well aware, Moses covered his face with a veil. It is because the people were afraid to talk to Moses, due to the shining glory of God on the face of Moses.

"When Aaron and all the Israelite saw Moses, his face was radiant, and they were afraid to come near him." (Exodus 34:30)

Why was the glory shining on the face of Moses? The glory shining on his face was a result of experiencing the glory of God.

"But whenever he entered the LORD'S presence to speak with him, he removed the veil until he came out. And when he came out and told the Israelite what he had been commanded, they saw that his face was radiant. Then Moses would put the veil back over his face until he went in to speak with the LORD." (Exodus 34:34-35)

Moses always entered the Most Holy Place to talk with God. The veil was removed when Moses entered the Most Holy Place, and the veil was placed back when outside. The veil was put on because the people were afraid of the Lord's glory. Moses prayed the prayer of the spirit at the Most Holy Place.

Do not think that the prayer of spirit is exclusive. The prayer of the spirit is about experiencing the Glory of God. The prayer is fulfilled with the Holy Spirit. God only receives the spiritual prayers, therefore when we pray the prayer of the spirit, we experience the Glory of God. Moses knew how to experience the glory of God. That is why he entered the Most Holy Place habitually, to experience the glory of God.

Moses' prayer in experiencing the glory of God is very similar to the prayer of Jesus. This can also be identified through the prayer of Peter and Paul. The only difference between the New Testament prayer and Moses' prayer relies upon the Most Holy Place. Only Moses was allowed to enter the Old Testament's Most Holy Place. Not even the high priest Aaron was allowed to enter the Most Holy Place (Leviticus 16:2). He was only allowed to enter the Most Holy Place on the 10th of July.

However, because of Jesus's death, we are all able to approach the Most Holy Place. The Most Holy Place is not only exclusive to the high priests. Anyone can experience the Glory of God. The Lord has opened the way for us.

"by a new and living way opened for us through the curtain, that is, his body" (Hebrews 10:20)

The tabernacle of Moses does not exist anymore. There no longer is the temple that was built over the 7-year period by Solomon. No more temple of Zerubbabel, or the temple of Herod. The only temple that remains is us. The temple of the Old Testament has crumbled down, but the bodies of the believers have been transformed into a temple today.

"Don't you know that you yourselves are God's temple, and that God's spirit lives in you?" (1Corinthians 3:16)

Now, we can enter the temple on daily basis. Also, the Most Holy Place can be entered without restrictions. We all can talk with God and experience the glory of God.

But, no one would claim that this is an easy task. It is tough to walk with the Holy Spirit and lean on his voice, despite our bodies being a temple. Why is it that hearing the voice of God is so tough? It is because we do not pray the prayer of the Spirit.

The prayer of the spirit is essential in walking with God. Why so? It is because God walks with us in his spirit.

"God is the spirit, and his worshipers must worship in the spirit and in truth." (John 4:24)

Basically, if we do not approach him in spirit, God does not abide with us in Spirit because God is with us in spirit. We must realize that if we are still being tossed back and forth by the worldly passions in our own knowledge and will, then God cannot be with us. The reason is simple. God is with us in spirit. Despite God's love for us, God, as the spirit, does not dwell with us in worldly ways. The problem is not with God, but with you. You must change. No more demanding that God should change. Obedience is our responsibility, and you must follow through. We know so many people in the Old Testament having prayed the prayer of the spirit.

There would not be enough time to mention them all. Was there such a prophet who did not incline to the voice of God? Perhaps, not among the fallen prophets. But a real prophet of God had to listen to God and walk with God in the spirit. It was the same case for Elijah and Elisha, also the same for Isaiah and Jeremiah. There are many more people than we know, who accompanied God in the spirit, who has not been recognized.

Countless people offered up the prayer of the spirit but the church of today is not interested in such a prayer anymore. The prayer of the spirit is not a special praying method, nor is it based on man made traditions. It is about praying to God in the spirit, who is Spirit. This is the method and this is the secret. Hear the voice of God through the prayer of the spirit. See the visions through the prayer of the spirit. Learn to walk with God through the prayer of The spirit. Your life will begin to experience the heavenly realm and your faith will experience a tremendous growth.

6) The prayer of the Spirit in New Testament

The people who prayed the prayer of the spirit are seldom found in the New Testament. The Holy Spirit's manifestation became possible after the Pentecost. Strangely enough, the Bible does not mention the people having walked with the Holy Spirit. Is it because these things happened without being mentioned? Regardless, it is not easy to trace back the footsteps of those who prayed the prayer of the spirit.

The prayer Jesus mentions is the prayer of the spirit. It is probable that Peter, Jesus' top disciple, prayed the prayer of the spirit. Some of his prayers are mentioned. One of them is Acts 10.

"About noon the following day as they were on their journey and approaching the city, Peter went up on the roof to pray. He became hungry and wanted something to eat, and while the meal was being prepared, he fell into a trance. He saw heaven open and something like a large sheet being let down to earth by its four corners. It contained all kinds of four-footed animals, as well as reptiles of the earth and birds of the air." (Acts 10:9-12)

Luke utilized the word "trance" in his recording of the book "Acts." What does the word, "trance" mean? "Trance" in Greek is "ekstasis." Amazingly, English utilizes the Greek word in its direct translation form. In English, it is called "ecstasy." This means "rapturous delight," "overpowering emotion" or "intense emotion of any kind." In most of the Bible translations, it is utilized as "trance." "Trance" also represents "a half-conscious state, seemingly between sleeping and walking", a "bewildered condition" or "unconscious condition".

At times, there are some who experience a rapture. We often label them as a "special" person. It is because not many are able to experience rapture. Those who have experienced it often say "the physical state of senses or consciousness could not be felt," or "the spirit was separated and was active apart from the body."

If you pray the prayer of the spirit, the state of rapture can be experienced. This is in parallel with Peter praying in a state of "trance." This differs from the prayer of petition and loud cries. It only prays in The spirit, as the prayer of the spirit. When the prayer of the spirit is carried out, the senses of the body are lost to a degree. This degree differs by the depth and level of the prayer.

Paul, often recognized as the pillar of the gentiles, also prayed the prayer of the spirit. Thankfully, Luke observed Paul's prayer very closely. Let's take a look at the prayer of Paul through Luke.

"When I returned to Jerusalem and was praying at the temple, I fell into a trance." (Acts 22:17)

Within this verse, the word "trance" (while in ecstasy) is used. In the New Testament, the word 'ecstasy' is used only twice. One is during the prayer of Peter and the other prayer of Paul.

There are reasons behind these two Apostles for having displayed such mighty works and power. It is a spiritual prayer, these prayers in Spirit work through might in power. Jesus also prayed "spiritual prayers". As known, Jesus prayed at a solitude place, not once but always did so. It is shown, how Jesus loved praying at a solitude place in Mark 1:35.

"Very early in the morning, while it was still dark, Jesus got up, left the house and went off to a solitary place, where he prayed" (Mark 1:35)

Jesus always chose solitary places and prayed alone. The following verse may explain as to why Jesus prayed alone.

"But when you pray, go into your room, close the door and pray to your Father, who is unseen. Then your Father, who sees what is done in secret, will reward you." (Matthew 6:6)

"Secret place" in Greek is "tamei'on". This can be translated as "your room" or "secret place". The reason for praying inside the secret place was explained by Jesus. "Then your Father, who sees what is done in secret, will reward you."

Jesus knows the characteristics of the prayer. If we come to realize the characteristics of Jesus' prayer, then the secrets of prayer will be revealed. It is because Jesus received all the power needed in his ministry through the prayer.

"How God anointed Jesus of Nazareth with the The Holy Spirit and power, and how he went around doing good and healing all who were under the power of the devil, because God was with him." (Acts 10:38)

If Jesus had not prayed, then the power of God could not be manifested. Jesus is 100% God, but at the same time was 100% man. Not even once did Jesus use the power of God, but only for us who live on the earth. Jesus received the power of God through prayer. The power in driving out demons and healing sicknesses were all received through prayer. That is why Jesus said "This kind can come out only by prayer."(Mark 9:29)

It is also possible for us. Why wouldn't it be? If we pray in the spirit, we can be like Peter and Paul.

Jesus prayed alone through his lifetime. Even at the garden of Gethsemane, Jesus set his disciples aside and prayed until his sweat turned into blood. But there was an exception. Only at this scene, Jesus prayed together with his disciples.

We call this the mount of transfiguration. It was not called a mount of transfiguration until the transfiguration did occur.

"About eight days after Jesus said this, he took Peter, John and James with him and went up onto a mountain to pray. As he was praying, the appearance of his face changed, and his clothes became as bright as a flash of lightning."(Luke 9:28-29)

I did not know the reason in Jesus's transfiguration and his clothes shining white, but I soon realized the reason after having prayed in the spirit. Jesus was transfigured because he prayed in the spirit.

We do not possess any information on Jesus' behavior and language regarding prayer, but we do know that the authority, power in action, and the love shown were all attained through prayer. The reason of Jesus taking his disciples to the mount of transfiguration was to teach them the true meaning of prayer.

Similar experiences in transfiguration can be felt in reality through praying in the spirit. The appearance of Jesus's transfiguration cannot be known in detail, but some special flow of energy does occur during the prayer of the spirit near the hands and head. Perhaps, the sick being healed through the handkerchief of Paul is in a similar line with Jesus' clothes shining in white.

"so that even handkerchiefs and aprons that had touched him were taken to the sick, and their illnesses were cured and the evil spirits left them." (Acts 19:12)

I believe in the healing ministry of Paul. I am a witness to similar ministries. Even now, the ministry of Paul continues through the Ministers of the Spirit.

Many pastors believe in the continuance of the Acts. Many believers profess this as well. If the book of Act is written with the purpose on continuance, the miracles of Paul must also be continued. The miracle of Deacon Philip turning an entire area of Samaria through the Gospel, and Peter raising the dead must be continued. Who dares to decide which is possible and which is impossible? Be aware of those who preach selectively in delivering the Gospel. We must follow the Bible. If Jesus prayed in solitude, then we must pray like him. If Jesus said to pray in a secret place, we must follow. If Paul's handkerchief healed, then our clothes must also reflect the power of healing. As the shadow of Peter healed, the sick must also be healed when we are near. Isn't this what we profess, and shouldn't it be an important part of our faith?

Chapter 2

....

Enter the Ark of the covenant

1. Power of the Tabernacle Prayer

A pastor, who had long been conducting seminars on the tabernacle, commented on our "tabernacle prayer". "It is amazing to know that one can pray through the tabernacle. Such a thought never occurred to me." Actually, there are a lot of seminars on tabernacle. But, these types of seminars are mostly involved in introducing the structures and the relics of the tabernacle, or providing a just enough guidance to live out a tabernacle-centered life. What the Holy Spirit has taught me through the tabernacle prayer differed widely from that of current seminars on the tabernacle.

One day, the Holy Spirit told me to make an internet café, which was a surprise, but due to the training and results gained during the encounter at the Tabernacle prayer, I was not alarmed. With obedience, the internet café was soon constructed, but without any major content. I felt stuck and asked the Holy Spirit what needed to be done next.

'Holy Spirit, the website is ready but what content should be there?'

The Holy Spirit told me to place all the papers I had written and commanded me to do nothing more. So I posted all the papers on the café. To my amazement, people began to visit the café and soon they began experiencing changes. The content in the café quenched their thirst and they expressed a great joy.

Then, the readers asked to be guided through the tabernacle prayer. So, I started guiding them through the tabernacle prayer. By utilizing an internet phone, the prayer sessions could last a long time without costing a single penny. The internet phone tabernacle prayer brought about a great change in its participants. In such a short time, they began to hear the voice of God and experienced an opening up of visions. As time progressed, more people began to gather through the internet café and they all needed to be lead through the tabernacle prayer.

I had to ask the Holy Spirit regarding this issue, and the Holy Spirit told me to guide the tabernacle prayer through the internet. I had to figure out how to serve the needs of so many people together through the internet tabernacle prayer. The answer was found in 'Skype'. Skype is free and up to 25 people can participate in a single call. Even though we couldn't see each other, the benefits of spiritual training were tremendous.

Within a short time of 5 months in opening up of an internet café, the numbers began to exceed 1,500 members. They all prayed together through the tabernacle prayer, and those who participated in the spiritual training exceeded 250. Nearly 20 tabernacle-prayer leaders were established and about 20 teams prayed at set times throughout the world. The tabernacle prayer session usually lasts 1 hour and 30 minutes. The time from the entrance of the tabernacle to arrival at the Ark of the

Covenant takes well over 1 hour. Truth be told, even for a person who exerts much effort in praying, experiences a tough time in passing the 1 hour mark. But in tabernacle prayer, the 1 hour mark feels as if only 10 minutes have passed by. These are not just my words but the words of those who pray the tabernacle prayer.

Many effects can be seen and felt through the tabernacle prayer, which do not involve any laying of hands or other special methods. It is unique in that the effects are experienced by anyone who prays the tabernacle prayer. They usually include a flow of electricity. This happens through the hands, feet, and the entire body. At times, a paralyzing effect occurs. At times, a heat wave will rise upward from the head. A feeling of oil dripping off of the entire body is another. Even a painful sensation of hands, wrist, and elbow, as if being cut off, can be felt. Over all, there are about 12 different categories of effects.

These effects begin to appear at the starting stage of the tabernacle prayer. Some do experience extreme cases of effect at the Altar of Burnt Offering through giving up of the flesh and soul. Others experience them while praying in tongues. But the real extreme effects can be experienced at the most holy place.

Visions open up very quickly at the most holy place. Most of the attendees meet the Lord hanging on the cross or some have conversation with him. Some even carry on the conversations by taking a journey on with the Lord. It was witnessed that carrying on the conversations helped in naturally hearing the voice of God.

At the Ark of the Covenant, the three relics inside help in experiencing the realities of God in depth. The stone tablet, budded staff and the jar of manna all represent a unique meaning. The stone tablet stands for the Covenant, while the budded staff represents faith, and the jar of manna resembles love. The participants of the tabernacle prayer are getting to know God more through the three relics.

What is more surprising in the Ark of the Covenant is experiencing God's glory. With the gates of heaven open, the cloud of God's glory envelops the praying person and the Lord's healing ray of light begins to shine down, which heals the sicknesses of the flesh and mind; or the fire of the Holy Spirit begins to manifest that which gives birth to many different gifts.

These kinds of extraordinary miracles happen through the tabernacle prayer. Many who follow the procedures by simply reading through them achieved these results. But, it is still recommended that a person should get assigned to a tabernacle prayer team and grow accountability on visions, hearing voices and prayer, which are the processes that help in maintaining a healthy spiritual training.

Normally, it would take 2 to 3 months of consistent participation in tabernacle prayers in hearing the voice of the Holy Spirit and seeing visions. Even children of 10 years of age and under have experienced opening up of visions and in hearing the voice of God simply by participating in the tabernacle prayer. Recently, an addition of the tabernacle prayer for the teens has been made. Also, to serve in sharing the tabernacle prayer world wide, an English tabernacle prayer class has become available.

1) Tabernacle prayer

Since the first day of talking with the Holy Spirit, he has spoken these words 'enter into the Ark of the Covenant'. There was no real knowledge about the Ark of the Covenant, I only knew that the most holy place carried it. Furthermore, not one person had elaborated on the Ark of the Covenant due to the lack of information in the Bible. Many books were sought after, but nothing of worth could be obtained.

But the Holy Spirit told me to enter into the Ark of the Covenant every time I began to pray. And with the guidance of the Holy Spirit, a vast amount of knowledge and experience accumulated in many years of time. There was no addition of man's knowledge or a single volume of book during this course of time. Only by leading of the Holy Spirit, an understanding on the "tabernacle prayer", "Ark of the Covenant Prayer" and "spiritual prayer" began to be known.

What the Holy Spirit wants through the 'tabernacle prayer' and the 'Ark of the Covenant prayer' and the 'prayer of the spirit', is the healing of relationships between the people of the earth and God. Prayer is about growing in a relationship with God. The greatest value of prayer is the mending of the relationship with God. Without prayer, there is no relationship with God. By ceasing the pray, one would only know God superficially.

The 'tabernacle prayer' can even be prayed by recent converts. However, the 'Ark of the Covenant prayer' or the 'prayer of the spirit' only applies to those with a high spiritual maturity. This does not mean that one must attend church for a long time. There are people who had not attended church for a long time yet possess a burning desire to maintain a strong relationship with God. But to those who attend church for a long time and are at a high position, yet they do not possess a heart for God, they are not worthy of the 'Ark of the Covenant prayer' or the 'prayer of the spirit' or even the 'tabernacle prayer'. It is because they are not interested in the spiritual affairs.

When I enter into a prayer, it begins with a request. "Holy Spirit, lead my prayer". In those times, the Holy Spirit leads my prayer. If the Holy Spirit says "make petition", then I make requests for petition if "pray in tongues" is heard, then a prayer in tongues is lifted up. "Should you not need more repentance?" then I spend more time repenting. When the Holy Spirit leads prayers, it lasts easily more than an hour. The prayers that feel like 20 minutes exceed an hour of prayer in reality. This was not only felt on me, but are held in common by everyone who prays the 'tabernacle prayer'.

The moment in understanding the processes of the 'tabernacle prayer' occurred through a healing revival and seminars in LA accompanied by the minister training sessions. I felt the need to pass on the prayer that is led by the Holy Spirit in me but did not know how. It is easy to mimic or make alterations to an already existing content. But, these prayers were not done or prayed by anyone. Because of this, it was hard to pass them on to others.

It was then that the knowledge of the 'tabernacle prayer' was finally grasped. I had already been praying the "tabernacle prayer" for a long while, so it was easy to understand what the Holy Spirit was saying. From then on, the knowledge of the 'tabernacle prayer' given by the Holy Spirit began to take effect, which allowed the prayer be prayed by everyone in the training session. Yes, there are certain frameworks that make up the 'tabernacle prayer', but these undergoes all require the leadership of the Holy Spirit. That is why the endless possibilities came about through the framework in the 'tabernacle prayer'. These possibilities did not depend on the participant's spiritual level or attitude. It did not rely on the frames of the prayer, but by the leadership of the Holy Spirit through the tabernacle prayer that created many changes in the spiritual state of its participants.

That is why the leading person of the "tabernacle prayer" must be a person who inclines to the voice of the Holy Spirit. It is possible to follow the steps of the 'tabernacle prayer'. It is even possible to carry the prayer out in a personalized manner or follow the pastor's specified steps. Even by merely following the steps mentioned in later chapters, many outstanding changes will be brought about from your prayer. Do know that a prayer lead by the Holy Spirit brings an experience of unfathomable grace and power.

When the time comes for you to hear and understand the voice of the Holy Spirit, these comments will begin to make sense. A prayer is not a solo, one-way communication. It is about the two-way communication. When the Holy Spirit speaks, I listen; not only listen, but ask questions as well. Then, question the need of why, only by then, will the communication process mature. These communications are not just involving the weather conditions or greetings. This communication is with the Holy Spirit, who even knows the deep thoughts of mankind. It is serious, delightful and full of unending joy. A very good and overflowing real joy.

I bring to you the 'tabernacle prayer' for those who desire to carry an intimate conversation with the Holy Spirit. Through the 'tabernacle prayer', your prayer depth will grow deep. The 3rd dimension prayer will turn into a 4th dimension prayer. The prayer of the soul will turn into a prayer of the spirit. The one-way conversation prayer will turn into a two-way communication prayer.

It is my hope and prayer that you will experience an enriching prayer life through this book. Hallelujah!

2. The Process of the Tabernacle Prayer

The tabernacle is important in reflecting the life of heaven. The author of Hebrews speaks of the tabernacle's amazing foreshadowing attributes.

"They serve as a sanctuary that is a copy and shadow of what is in heaven. This is why Moses was warned when he was about to build the tabernacle: "See to it that you make everything according to the pattern shown you on the mountain." (Hebrews 8:5)

When God spoke to Moses in building the tabernacle, it was to show him the heavenly things. It is because the tabernacle is a 'shadow of what is in heaven'. Just as the priests serve God at the tabernacle, there will be worshiping of God in heaven. As the tabernacle purified the sins of all the people, there will be a continuance of living in purity through the tabernacle in heaven.

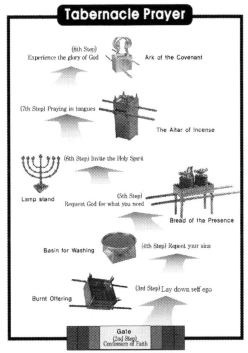

Tabernacle Prayer

(8th Step)
Experience the glory of God

Ark of the Covenant

(7th Step) Praying in tongues

The Altar of Incense

(6th Step) Invite the Holy Spirit

Lamp stand

(5th Step)
Request God for what you need

Bread of the Presence

Basin for Washing

(4th Step) Repent your sins

(3rd Step) Lay down self ego

Burnt Offering

Gate
(2nd Step)
Confession of Faith

(1st Step) Sprinkle the blood of Jesus

Life in heaven revolves around worshiping. It is about walking with God eternally. The people will gather around to worship in heaven. There will be a tabernacle to worship and praise God in Heaven.

"And I heard a loud voice from the throne saying, now the dwelling of God is with men, and he will live with them. They will be his people, and God himself will be with them and be their God." (Revelations 21:3)

For those who hate to worship will undergo a burdensome life in heaven. Those who dislike praying, their life in heaven will also be boring. Heaven is about focusing on God only, who becomes our devotion and our only purpose of servitude. We will be a people of God and he will be our God.

God had us build the tabernacle, so that those on earth would live in a preparation for heaven. He has shown us how to pray and worship Him appropriately through the tabernacle.

Time has come for me to share with you in detail about praying through the tabernacle.

At the starting stage of the tabernacle prayer, rely on the Lord and begin to sprinkle the blood of the Lord. When training the Leaders, I recommend sprinkling the blood three times on each part of the body: head, face, chest, stomach, reproductive organs and the knees. By performing the task of sprinkling the Lord's blood before commencing a prayer, attacks of the demons can be defended. There is a vast difference between where the blood has been sprinkled and where it has not been.

It is also important to sprinkle the Lord's blood around the prayer location before the prayer begins. When I pray at church, the sprinkling of Lord's blood is done from the entrance and all around. The proclaiming and sprinkling of the Lord's blood is done by shouting "Blood of Jesus!"

"Sprinkling of the Lord's blood, be purified!"

"Sprinkling of the Lord's blood, Depart filthy and vile the spirits!"

Some places are spiritually dark, especially an old building, or places that had hosted an immoral business practices in being renovated to be a place for a church. Regardless, by the sprinkling of the Lord's blood and through prayers, the evil spirits will not be able to come near it. However, it doesn't mean an absolute disappearance. With a repetition of sprinkling the Lord's blood and a continued prayer in the same location, it will turn into a holy ground that will drive away the influence of evil spirits.

Even at home, it is good to pick out a place and pray there, if possible. Jesus tells us to pray in a 'secret place' (Matthew 6:6). The secret place is where there is no disruption from others. The smaller the place, the better it is. Because, when the Lord's blood is sprinkled, the manifestation of power becomes stronger especially in smaller places. That is why the leaders hear these words, "if there is no sufficient place, go inside a car and do it."

The Lord's blood is very important from the start of tabernacle prayer to the end. The tremendous authority of the Lord's blood will soon be experienced.

1) Through the Tabernacle Gate

The tabernacle gate is knitted by twisting blue, purple, scarlet and white linen. The tabernacle gate represents the Lord. The blue color speaks of Jesus as the life. The purple represents Jesus as the king. The color scarlet shows the suffering of Jesus. The resurrection of Jesus is presented with the white.

In order to pray the tabernacle prayer, there must be a continuing reliance on the Lord. It is because the Lord is "the way, the truth and life" (John 14:16). As previously mentioned, imagine yourself standing at the tabernacle gate, after having sprinkled the Lord's blood on the body and the prayer location. Eagerly anticipate at the gate of the tabernacle opening through the power of Jesus. You must confess the four fulfillment of Jesus so that the tabernacle gate will open up. Make sure to confess by the speaking out through the mouth. Then, in due time, the door will open up and you will witness yourself entering into the tabernacle.

Passing through the tabernacle gate is the first stage in accepting Jesus as the savior and making confessions of faith with your mouth. (Refer to John 1:12).

If you are leading the tabernacle prayer, tell the participants to imagine them selves standing at the tabernacle gate. Then, the participants of prayer will close their eyes and begin to imagine standing in front of the tabernacle gate. And, Jesus' four fulfillment must be followed by explanations. Do not spend a lot of time here. It can simply be read out with statements written below. And this is okay. But, try to have the four fulfillment of Jesus memorized(with scriptures) in reciting them to the participants during the tabernacle prayer.

First, Jesus is God, who is life. Jesus grants us life. Whoever believes and follows Jesus attains life. Many follow the ways of the world, but there is no life in it. The world only grants us the cravings of the flesh. Jesus is the only life.

"When Christ, who is your life, appears, then you also will appear with him in glory." (Colossians 3:4)

Second, Jesus is God, who is King. David praised the King Jesus. David was a king, who had possessed the enlarged territory of Israel. It is a great feat for such a king to serve someone as their King. Do you serve Jesus as the king?

"I will exalt you, my God the King; I will praise your name for ever and ever." (Psalms 145:1)

Third, Jesus is God, who had suffered. Jesus suffered for your sake. He suffered for this very 'Me'. When an understanding of

Jesus having suffered for 'Me' takes place, the great love of Jesus will also be revealed.

When you are tired and weary, do not carry those burdens by yourself. Jesus has already taken all of your burdens. The Lord, himself has suffered and was tempted, so that he is able to help you with the temptations.

"Because he himself suffered when he was tempted, he is able to help those who are being tempted." (Hebrews 2:18)

Fourth, Jesus is God, who has resurrected. Jesus defeated death and became victorious. As Jesus triumphed over death, we can also overcome all our problems.

"but it has now been revealed through the appearing of our Savior, Christ Jesus, who has destroyed death and has brought life and immortality to light through the gospel." (2 Timothy 1:10).

2) Death of the Ego of Flesh, at the Altar of Burnt Offering

By entering through the tabernacle gate, an altar of burnt offering will be noticed at the courtyard of the tabernacle.

This place is where the commitment of devotion is made. Slay yourself at this place. Just as an animal is burnt up, witness yourself burn like the animal. Animals were slain at the tabernacle of Moses, but you must slay yourself on top of the altar of burnt offering through the prayer of the spirit.

Climb up the altar of burnt offering. As the fire begins to kindle, your flesh will burn away. Put an end to your ego of the flesh at this place. If the ego of the flesh is not dead, the glory of God cannot be manifested. The life in the flesh ego lessens the glory of God, these things will begin to disappear. Burn away your shameful self at the altar of burnt offering. The selfish desires with its bad behaviors, burn them all up. The thoughts that pretended it was all for God, when it was all for yourself, burn them up. Following the traditions of men, instead of following the will of God, burn up those misbehaviors.

Promise God that you will offer up your self wholly at the altar of burnt offering. Confess in such a way like this.

"I am wholly yours."

"I will live only for you Lord."

"I offer up my flesh and mind for you Lord."

The Lord will delight in these confessions and build up your faith to a greater depth. The context below is an expanded explanation. If you are a leader of a tabernacle prayer session, memorize the information below, and recite it to the participants at the altar of burnt offering.

You are already a temple of God (1 Corinthians 3:16). What does it say concerning the temple and the dweller of the Temple?

"Don't you know that you yourselves are God's temple and that God's spirit lives in you?" (1 Corinthians 3:16)

Correct. The Holy Spirit dwells within us. This has already been obtained by us through the baptism of the Holy Spirit. As the Apostle Paul mentioned, the baptism of the Holy Spirit is received by confessing that Jesus is the Christ and that God raised him from the dead (Romans 10:9). After the baptism of the Holy Spirit, the Holy Spirit dwells within us. As stated, baptism of the Holy Spirit turns our body into a temple.

What doesn't make sense is that the Holy Spirit dwelling in us never actually shows up. Who is the Holy Spirit? He is God. God lives in our body but we do not see any powers of God or even the holy attributes of God. How can this be?

This is because our ego of flesh is still persisting. Our ego of the flesh must be put to death in order that the Holy Spirit will be able to manifest. Paul spoke with these words "I die everyday" (1 Corinthians 15:30). The life of Paul was full of the Holy Spirit's manifestation. He shares how the Holy Spirit can be manifested.

"I have been crucified with Christ and I no longer live, but Christ lives in me. The life I live in the body, I live by faith in the Son of God, who loved me and gave himself for me." (Galatians 2:20).

We must nail our ego of the flesh to the cross. Being crucified is about getting rid of my flesh ego. Only then, the Holy Spirit within us will be able to manifest itself and bring out the life of Christ.

3) Prayer of Purity at the Wash Basin

If you are one of the leaders for the tabernacle prayer, continue to encourage the participants in committing at the altar of burnt offering through prayer. The participants will begin to express out their commitments to the Lord. They will pray to get rid of the flesh ego. Rather than the repentance of sins, this prayer will become a stepping stone in giving oneself wholly to the Lord, for the glory of the Lord.

As the prayer at the altar of burnt offering comes to an end, lead the participants toward the wash basin.

Once arriving at the Wash Basin, give a description of the wash basin. Remember that the Wash Basin is one of the only relics that make no mention of its size. The size is not mentioned, because the each participant's amount of repentance differs. It should be clear that, without fully washing our sins clean, no one will be able to approach the holy place.

As we make commitments at the altar of burnt offering, next step is wash basin leading to repentance of sins. A time of repentance is a must. Many think that there is nothing to repent about. This cannot be true. If one says that there is nothing to repent, than that person is already standing in a worse situation. 'Pride' has a hold on that individual. Nothing is more dangerous, and this should require all the more repentance.

When a true repentance comes, your eyes will shed tears and your nose will start to run. Without the tears of repentance, one cannot experience the true repentance. Just because the tears of repentance were shed once, it does not mean that the repentance is completed. Take the time to repent in every prayer session.

Do you recall the time when David repented to God concerning his adultery with Bathsheba? All of our sins have been committed against God first. Even if the sin was committed against a person, the sin is committed against God who has created us. The sin that was done against me is also committed against God first. The sins were committed against God, the creator. So, always seek God first and confess your sins through repentance. After that, ask for the forgiveness of those who we have sinned against and make a restitution.

Consider this, longer and more fervent time spent in repenting will yield in a greater and deeper grace of God.

The following is an additional explanation. The leaders must be able to recite this information. This context will provide additional help in guiding during the prayers.

We have been set free from the 'one trespass'. Through the redemption of the Lord's cross, our trespass has been abolished. All the results of sin through Adam were paid in full.

"For just as through the disobedience of the one man the many were made sinners, so also through the obedience of the one man the many will be made righteous." (Roman 5:19)

Through Jesus, the trespass of Adam was casted away and it cannot lay hold on us anymore! Hallelujah! But we continue to sin. This speaks of the individual's sins. Although the inherited sin is broken, if there remain the sins of an individual; those sins must be repented. Without it, one cannot become pure. Sins must be repented when approaching God.

Repent of these sins through the everyday prayer of the tabernacle. Lay down all sins at the foot of the cross. Repent the sins done against the husband and wife. Repent the sins done against the parents and children. Repent of sins committed against brothers and sisters. Repent the vile and shameful sins. Repent of all the sins that you are aware of. Even the sins that cannot be recognized, repent. By the help of the Holy Spirit, repentance can be made. If possible, do it with sincerity. At least, Repent with a loud wailing and on your knees. The amazing grace of our Lord will purify us from our sins and give peace to our minds.

"If we confess our sins, he is faithful and just and will forgive us our sins and purify us from all unrighteousness." (1 John 1:9)

4) Petition at the Bread of Presence

You have been purified, if repentance was fulfilled at the wash basin. Now, approach the holy place with confidence. The holy place is covered by the tent. This tent is layered with four different linens. This represents a territory that has been set apart. However, the tent has been set apart once again within the tabernacle.

Anyone can reside within the courtyard of the tabernacle. In that place, a commitment is made after the repentance of sins. The altar of burnt offering and wash basin does this job specifically. As the altar of burnt offering stands for the baptism of the Holy Spirit, the wash basin represents the water baptism and baptism of the Holy Spirit's fire. And, even if the baptism of the Holy Spirit and water baptism was received through the altar of burnt offerings and the wash basin, it is still too early to be called as a true worshiper. A worshiper becomes a true one when entering the holy place within the tent. If you are one of the tabernacle prayer leaders, speak of these things to the participants. "Now, your flesh has been purified. With this permission, it is time to approach the Holy place with a confidence."

Then, the people will begin to enter in their minds to the holy place.

Once entering the holy place, the three relics can be noticed. Right side (from our perspective) is placed with the bread of presence, the left side holds the golden lamp stand and the space in between the most holy place and the holy place resides the altar of incense.

Look to the bread of presence. (tell them to look up at the Bread of Presence). The bread of presence represents Jesus as life. The bread laid on the table is about relying on the Lord, who provides our daily needs and responds to our petitions. In that very place, our petitions are lifted up. It involves an intercessory prayer that prays for the family and for our selves. Even the smallest things must be petitioned in request during the prayer.

This process includes petitions accompanied by declarations. A majority of the people only do petitions. But when the petitions are followed by declarations, the responses will be very quick. For example, if the petition was done like this, "God, please heal my son's sickness," then it must be accompanied with "In the name of Jesus of Nazareth, I command, the spirit of sickness that is bothering my son ... Depart at this very hour!" Declare it in such a way.

This moment involves our usual prayers accompanied by a declaration, which will bring amazing results. This process may take more than ten minutes.

The following information is an additional content for referencing. Please be informed.

The altar of burnt offering and the Wash Basin were conducted as preparation for the praising of God. If the ego does not die at the altar of burnt offering or if the sin is not repented at the wash basin, it is impossible to praise him.

The bread of presence represents Jesus as our daily bread. In this very hour, ask God about your needs. Make petitions for your very own family.

"Then Jesus declared, "I am the bread of life. He who comes to me will never go hungry, and he who believes in me will never be thirsty." (John 6:35)

"If you remain in me and my words remain in you, ask whatever you wish, and it will be given you." (John 15:7)

"Until now you have not asked for anything in my name. Ask and you will receive, and your joy will be complete." (John 16:24)

5) Inviting the Holy Spirit at the Golden Lamp Stand.

Invite the Holy Spirit at the golden lamp stand. What we must remember is that the opening up of the tabernacle prayer was begun in the name of the Lord. The full armoring was done through the blood of the Lord, commitments were made to the Lord, and the Lord forgave us our sins. Furthermore, our needs were petitioned through declaring in the name of the Lord. All the prayer contents share a relation to the Lord.

But the time at the golden lamp stand is a time to rely on the Holy Spirit. It is because from this point on the prayer of spirit needs a time of preparation. And the prayer time spent means experiencing the glory of God.

Inviting the Holy Spirit means the Holy Spirit in you is becoming active through the power of the spirit. It doesn't mean inviting the Holy Spirit who resides in others, or bringing it from a different location. You will be asking the Holy Spirit residing in you to start working in you.

"Thank you Holy Spirit. Reign over me this very moment."

"Guide me Holy Spirit, so that I may be able to experience the glory of God."

As you begin to pray like this, the Holy Spirit will start to guide you into the most holy place.

If you are leading the tabernacle prayer, explain the above contents to the participants. After that, follow the steps instructed below.

"Thank you Holy Spirit. Reign over me this very moment."

"Guide me Holy Spirit, so that I may be able to experience the Glory of God."

Speak the lines above, and then encourage the participants to start feeling the Holy Spirit, who is accompanying the group. The people will actually feel the Holy Spirit's accompanying presence. The acknowledgment of the Holy Spirit accompanying you will help greatly in the next step of prayer at the altar of incense.

The following is a reference material. Please be advised.

The manifestation of the Holy Spirit can only be shown by restricting our 'self'. The Holy Spirit is made manifest when our ego dies. We must get rid of self, our very self, so that the Holy Spirit can walk with us. Only then can we walk with the Holy Spirit. If there is a sin, we cannot walk with him, because the sin separates our relationship from God.

"But your iniquities have separated you from your God; your sins have hidden his face from you, so that he will not hear." (Isaiah 59:2)

But, when I disappear and the Holy Spirit remains, the sins will vanish. The Holy Spirit turns us into being holy and pure. The Holy Spirit will fulfill the entry of the most holy place in experiencing the glory of God.

6) Prayer at the Altar of Incense

The altar of incense is a very important relic. In Hebrews chapter 9, the altar of incense is placed inside the most holy place (See Hebrews 9:3-4). This is because the book of Hebrews is recorded based upon the tabernacle that is in heaven. As the tabernacle in the book of Exodus is based on the earthly one, the book of Hebrews is based on the heavenly tabernacle. Some bible scholars profess that the book of Hebrews is one of the hardest books to comprehend, because they cannot hear the voice of the Holy Spirit and are unable to see the tabernacle that is in heaven. If one had seen the heavenly tabernacle or has heard the voice of God, the book of Hebrews would be one of the easiest books to understand.

The heavenly tabernacle contains only the altar of incense, the Ark of the Covenant and the atonement cover placed on top of the Ark of the Covenant. In that place, the Gate of the Tabernacle, the altar of burnt offering, the wash basin, the bread of the presence, or the golden lampstand isn't there. There is no sin in heaven. It is a place for the gathering of people, who are committed to devotion, therefore the relics such as the Altar of Burnt Offerings or the Wash Basin are no longer needed. Also, the bread of presence and the golden lampstand are not needed, because the Holy Spirit will always walk with us. That is why the Altar of Incense is placed inside the most holy place. The altar of incense represents prayers. The earthly location needs prayers, as does the heavenly realm, and that is why the Altar of Incense is inside the Most Holy Place.

Now, be led by the Holy Spirit in praying at the altar of incense. What prayers should be offered? You have already requested the needs of the flesh and followed with declarations.

The answers to that prayer will soon be received. This stops at the bread of presence. It is because, until now, only the prayer of flesh and soul has been prayed.

Now, with the Holy Spirit's guidance (golden lamp stand), begin to pray at the altar of incense, but know that this is a very special prayer. It is the prayer of tongues. Paul encourages praying in tongues and is also one of the 9 gifts of the Holy Spirit. So just because you are unable to pray in tongues, do not treat the prayer of tongues as a cheap gift, it only creates a complication.

Paul refers to speaking in tongues as 'my spirit praying'. "For if I pray in a tongue, my spirit prays, but my mind is unfruitful" (1 Corinthians 14:14). Its tendencies in thinking that the prayer in tongues is solely involved with praying in spirit can be frequently seen. It is true that the praying in tongues is my spirit praying. But the prayer in tongues is not all that is in the prayer of the spirit.

When the prayer in tongues is prayed, we start it at our will. Yes, the receiving of tongues first happens through the major changes in our spirit, rather than in our will. But, after having received the gift of speaking in tongues, the praying in tongues can be started at will. I can speak in tongues whenever wanted. Even though the tongues can begin at will, as time progresses my spirit begins to grow and naturally begins to pray in the spirit. As such, speaking in tongues is a very precious gift that connects human souls to the spirit.

The Holy Spirit summarizes praying in tongues as a "Key to opening up the heavens." What must be remembered is, to give it your utmost effort when praying in tongues. Try doing so until your throat loses voice. Try doing it aloud. Try speaking fast. As speaking in tongues may begin with 'la la la,' when deep into the prayer, it returns to the 'la la la' stage. The importance is to give it your best.

The following includes additional descriptions of praying in tongues.

We must pray every day. Paul encourages prayer of tongues. "I thank God that I speak in tongues more than all of you" (1 Corinthians 14:18). It is very important that we pray in tongues. It is because the prayer in tongues is a 'key to opening up the heavens'. Paul talks about praying in tongues with these words.

"For if I pray in a tongue, the spirit prays, but my mind is unfruitful" (1 Corinthians 14:14).

Paul describes speaking in tongues as praying in the spirit. But it cannot be said that the prayer in tongues is all that the spiritual prayer involves. Praying in tongues is a preparation phase in being able to pray the prayer of the spirit. Just as the altar of incense is done in preparation of entering the most holy place, the prayer in tongues is done in preparation for the prayer of the spirit. The prayer of the spirit will naturally come through the prayer of tongues.

Do not bother listening to what the prayer of tongues is speaking. Only focus on the glory of God.

7) Sprinkling of Blood at the Most Holy Place

As the time passes, the exerted effort of praying in tongues will grow the spirit, but a peaceful feeling will also begin to seep in. It is that moment when the heavenly music can be heard, and the visitation of the Lord happens, or visions can accompany the voice of the Holy Spirit. Yes, you can talk with the Lord and even hear the voice of God. Do not think of the trinity God as one God. God as 3 different beings has an individual personality. You will gain a deeper understanding of the realities of God, Jesus and the Holy Spirit through the experiences.

As the peacefulness can be felt in the spirit, that place is the most holy place. You have just entered the most holy place and are standing in front of the Ark of the Covenant covering, which is the atonement cover. The blood of the Lord must be sprinkled once again. The ark of the Covenant contains the very presence of God. The glory of God can be experienced, only by entering the ark of the covenant. But there is a gate. That gate is the atonement cover. You must sprinkle the blood of the Lord on the atonement cover. Sprinkle the blood on your body as well.

The sprinkling of the blood was done with the hands at the start of the tabernacle prayer, but the sprinkling is done through the spirit at the atonement cover. Your hands do not perform any task. Your mouth does not open. The body remains still. Thoughts are stopped. There is no praise in this place. No prayer is spoken out loud. Only the spirit works. And you will experience the words of Romans 8:16.

When you sprinkle the blood of the Lord at the atonement cover, the two cherubs overshadowing the atonement cover will make way towards the Ark of the Covenant. You will pass by the cherubs that are protecting the Atonement Cover and enter into the Ark of the Covenant. Once inside the Ark of the Covenant, the spirit will be filled with great joy. The fullness of God's glory will be felt all around you.

If you are leading the tabernacle prayer, walk through the details above. However, if you are not able to hear the voice of the Holy Spirit, there will be difficulties in leading the prayer, as this part of the process cannot be explained or guided with the human will or by mere words. If you are able to hear the voice of the Holy Spirit, then people can be led by the voice of the Holy Spirit. When it is done, the prayer will become more fruitful in the spirit and that moment will lead many to experience the great glory of God. Yes, in that moment the voice of God will be heard and many will see visions by opening up of the spiritual eyes. Furthermore, the great power of God will be experienced.

Below entails an additional information, please consider the following.

As done previously, the blood of Jesus was also sprinkled at the beginning of the tabernacle prayer. If a secret place has been chosen for the tabernacle prayer, sprinkle the blood of Jesus whenever entering it. The high priests always sprinkled the blood, when entering the Most Holy Place.

"He is to take some of the bull's blood and with his finger sprinkle it on the front of the atonement cover; then he shall sprinkle some of it with his finger seven times before the atonement cover" (Leviticus 16:14).

Nobody can enter the most holy place without the Blood. Not one person can experience the glory of God without the blood of Jesus.

"Therefore, brothers, since we have confidence to enter the most holy place by the blood of Jesus" (Hebrews 10:19)

Although the blood of Jesus was sprinkled before the prayer, sprinkle it once again at the atonement cover.

Whenever the blood of Jesus is sprinkled, think of the cross. Visit the cross standing at the hill of Golgotha.

Stand at the cross of Jesus. Kneel at the feet of Jesus.

Feel the blood of Jesus dripping down his feet. Touch the cross that Jesus was hung on.

Touch the feet of Jesus. Place your hands inside the side of Jesus.

Look upon the face of Jesus.

Place the crown of thorns from Jesus to you. Instead of Jesus, go unto your cross.

This is the very sprinkling of the Jesus' blood. By sprinkling the blood of Jesus in this manner, you will see the gate of heaven opening up. You will deeply experience the glory of God.

8) The glory of God inside the Ark of the Covenant

The Ark of the covenant contains three relics: the stone tablet that is written with the commandments of God, Aaron's staff that had budded and the golden jar of manna (Hebrews 9:4). The stone tablet has all the written the covenants of God. This is called the covenant. It is a very good thing to think of God's words when experiencing the glory of God. When God speaks, he will speak the words according to the Bible.

Aaron's staff that had budded represents faith. This speaks of the faith as mentioned in "the God who gives life to the dead and calls things that are not as though they were" (Romans 4:17). Abraham knew that his body was as good as dead, but held on to the promise of God. God credited this to him as righteousness and he became the father of faith (See Romans 4 & Hebrews 11).

The golden jar of manna symbolizes the love of God. The love of God that loves me yesterday, today and tomorrow can be experienced.

As you remain in the Ark of the Covenant, you will experience the Covenant of God, the faith of God and the love of God. The things that concern these will be learned in detail. God is the God of the covenant. He keeps all the promises made to us. God is the God of faith. He offers a great faith to us. God is the God of love. Through the Ark of the Covenant prayer, your love will turn to that likeness of the love of God.

Also by remaining inside the Ark of the Covenant, the great glory and power of God will be made manifest. By staying inside the Ark of the Covenant, God's cloud of glory, Jesus' healing ray of light, and the fire of the Holy Spirit will be recognized. The opening up of the heaven's gate will be witnessed with some time passing by, and you will begin to feel the cloud of glory pouring down on you. As the cloud covers you, the fullness of God's glory will be felt. As the nose breathes in the glory of God, the pores of your body taking in the glory of God through the nose will be felt. All of your entire skin will begin to change as the cloud touches your skin. As some time is spent here, a bright ray of light will suddenly flash down from the heavens and penetrate straight through to your heart. The ray of light will continue to shine down upon it and soon will turn into a small spark of fire. The fire will go through your entire body and heal the aching parts of the body. The cancer cells will be burned; dirty and vile spirits will be burned. And in doing so, your body and mind will enjoy good health. The ray of light turning into a fire, and moving about the painful parts requires your faith. As the Lord's healing ray of light begins to heal your body, suddenly the fire of the Holy Spirit will burst forth from the very depths of you. At this moment, your body will begin to shake and the power of God will be made manifest to you.

You will undergo a great transformation through the continued prayer of the spirit. God will do amazing works. The conversation with the Holy Spirit will go on as the effects of the cloud and fire envelop around you through the prayers. Because your spirit has reached the good stage of growth, the voice of the Holy Spirit will be heard, enabling you to carry on a conversation.

There is no limit to the prayer of the spirit. Have you felt the two hours passing by as if ten minutes had gone by? The prayer of the spirit will do just that. This is possible in many times throughout the day. This is not done under compulsion, but is a delightful experience, because of the precious moments spent in talking and learning from God.

The prayer done inside the Ark of the Covenant cannot be explained in detail. These areas of contents cannot be understood in mere words. This must be experienced. The person, who cannot hear the voice of the Holy Spirit, cannot lead the prayer of the spirit. Because, inside the Ark of the Covenant, it is you that depend on the voice of the Holy Spirit for guidance. Actually, introducing the Ark of the Covenant prayer to a group of people who are not so passionate or have weak faith, even they end up experiencing the glory of God. How much more so for those who can hear the voice of the Holy Spirit and does pray the spiritual prayers! The Ark of the Covenant prayer captures a time of surpassing grace. Be sure to experience it.

The following entails additional information. Please read through it.

The pillar of fire and the pillar of cloud, that represents the glory of God, started with the Ark of the Covenant. It is because the Ark of the Covenant was a replica of the one that is in the temple of heaven. The apostle John saw the temple in heaven, and the temple contained the ark of the covenant.

"Then God's temple in heaven was opened, and within his temple was seen the ark of his the covenant. And there came flashes of lightning, rumblings, peals of thunder, an earthquake and a great hailstorm" (Revelations 11:19).

The temple in the heaven does not need anything else but the Ark of the Covenant. Because God has overpowered the dominion of demons by placing them inside the eternal hell, the citizens of heaven no longer can reside in sin. This is why that the altar of burnt offering and the Wash Basin is no longer needed. The bread of presence at the holy place is no longer needed. Why would the bread of presence be needed in heaven, when we are with the Lord everyday? The golden lamp stand will not be needed either. There is no reason to have the golden lamp stand, when we are walking with the Holy Spirit everyday. But the altar of incense is needed. The altar of incense and the most holy place relics are needed. The author of Hebrews must have understood these truths. To our amazement, the author says that the altar of incense is located inside the most holy place.

"Behind the second curtain was a room called the most holy place, which had the golden altar of incense and the gold-covered ark of the covenant. This ark contained the gold jar of manna, Aaron's staff that had budded, and the stone tablets of the covenant" (Hebrews 9:3-4)

Why did the tabernacle of Moses place the Altar of Incense at the holy place, while the author of Hebrews mentions that the altar of incense is at the most holy place? Author of Hebrews saw the tabernacle through the spirit. He saw it from the heavenly perspective. It is absolutely needed that the heavens contain the altar of incense. But the tabernacle of Moses had to have the altar of incense at the holy place. The altar of incense had to be kept burning 365 days a year. As we know, the most holy place could only be approached by the high priest, that only once a year on an atonement day. Anyone else would be dead by entering it.

If the altar of incense was placed inside the most holy place, how could you keep the incense burning everyday? It is right to have the altar of incense at the holy place. But with the heavenly perspective, it is also correct to have the altar of incense at the most holy place. That is why the words in the Bible are without a single error.

The glory of God is experienced by remaining inside the Ark of the Covenant. The glory of God shows up through the cloud and fire. As the gate of heaven opens up, the cloud that represents the glory of God will envelope you. When the cloud covers you, all the evil and filthy spirits within you will depart. The power of demons can no longer attack you. The cloud of glory will protect you.

There is another kind of glory aside from the cloud, which is the pillar of fire. The fire has three different characteristics. It burns, lights up and passes on. Jesus is the light that reveals the image of God. Jesus came as the light of the world.

"The Son is the radiance of God's glory and the exact representation of his being ......" (Hebrews 1:3)

"I have come into the world as a light, so that no one who believes in me should stay in darkness" (John 12:46).

When the light of Jesus shines down, the glory of God will come to you with a greater manifestation. Jesus is the healing ray of light (Malachi 4:2). You need to be focused on the light when it shines down upon you. As an effort is exerted in focusing on the light, that very light will turn into a small spark of fire. This is as if a magnifying glass is concentrating on the surrounding lights to burn a piece of paper. As such, when the fire is formed, move the fire around your infected parts. Focus on that fire. In no time, the infected area will begin to feel hot and you will begin to feel the healing in those areas. Like this, the Lord's light will heal your spirit, soul and pain and diseases in the flesh.

Another characteristic of fire is consuming. The fire of the Holy Spirit burns all the filth and gives you a power. The glory of God is the same; it will burn like the great consuming fire.

Meditate everyday on these three characteristics that represent the glory of God. The cloud, light and fire. Remember, this will give growth to your spirit and power.

3. I will enter the Ark of the Covenant

1) Enter the Ark of the Covenant

The Holy Spirit gave me these words. Until then, I had possessed no prior knowledge of the 'Ark of the covenant'. There was not even a notion of knowing the purpose in the Ark of the Covenant. I only knew that the Ark of the Covenant was placed inside the most holy place. That is why I could not grasp these words, "Enter the Ark of the covenant." The only viable option was to ask the Holy Spirit.

"Holy Spirit, how can one enter the Ark of the Covenant?"

The Holy Spirit began to explain in detail about the Ark of the Covenant. But this was not done in a span of a day. It took approximately 3 months to understand the finer details. There was some additional information gained at a later stage, but most of it was obtained in a 3 month period time.

Now, I will open up the doors of the tabernacle and describe it in depth, concerning the procedure from inside the tabernacle to entering the Ark of the Covenant in experiencing the glory of God. The following words will benefit many tabernacle prayer participants.

2) Tabernacle prayer at the secret place

The prayer that the Lord recommends is the prayer at the 'secret place' (See Matthew 6:6). The secret place is your very own 'secret place of the spirit'. Make note that the spirit of God interacts with your spirit only at the secret place of the spirit.

That is why the very first thing that needs to be done is to prepare the secret place of the spirit.

The 'secret place of the spirit' refers to the place where one can remain in solitude. A place that is crowded cannot be a real 'secret place,' but even if many are accompanying you, if that crowd prays the tabernacle prayer through its leader, that place can be used to prepare the 'secret place of the spirit'. Having a tough time in finding the 'secret place of the spirit' while being with someone is because of interruptions. If I am confessing silently, but the other person begins to confess by speaking out loud, your 'mind' will respond to it immediately. As a result, your 'spirit' will begin to drift. If I am entering the most holy place by finishing the prayer in tongues, but the person next to me continues to pray in tongues; my 'mind' will begin to be active again and react to the prayer.

If possible, it is important to be alone, considering the several things that can interfere with activating your spirit. Find a place where you can be alone in the flesh; a place where no interruptions can occur for at least an hour. If there is no such place, then visiting a church at an empty hour is just as well. Perhaps, it would be good to pray at an early or a late night hour.

The 'secret place of the spirit' has to be separated from the noise of the world. Your spirit can not become activate if there is background music. Some pray while listening to a sounding music, as if meditating through calmness embedded in its music. It is better to pray on a street where there is a fire truck blaring an alarm, rather than to pray with music in the background.

Forsaking background music is due to its characteristics. Music is spiritual. There are some who enjoy listening to classical music, but people deeply into classical music are surprisingly influenced in the spirit. That is why people who like classical music are very organized, clean and graceful. This is due to the influential characteristics of classical music

Music is like an idol. Before entering the seminary school, I had majored in music for over a 10-year period. The characteristics of music are well known to me. A church conductor can appear to be fervent in his spirit by an observation through his sweat and diligence. But it can result from an idolization. With a mere glimpse, that faith can appear to be healthy but in reality, that passion is from the heart yearning for more music.

I have stopped listening to a classical music. At times, some classical music may come to my ears, and it still drags me down to listening with a passion. The thought of 'what a great feeling' begins to emerge. That feeling is very similar to that of listening to a hymnal music. But there is a great difference. The truth is, classical music does not remind us of God. This is the destructive power in a worldly music.

I am reminded of a music CD called 'a prayer of meditation'. The music is very beautiful, yet calm, and assures its value in meditating. But now, that music has become an obstacle in praying the spiritual prayer. When I moved to an apartment in LA, a loud noise began to seep through the closet that had been renovated for a prayer space. The noise of cars passing by, grass- cutting noise and children playing outside interfered with my prayer. I played the music CD thinking that the music would drown out the noise.

Suddenly, the Holy Spirit commanded abruptly "Turn it off." Every time the 'prayer of meditation' CD was played during the prayer time, the Holy Spirit commanded to shut it off. This was a command that I could not come to terms with. There was no choice but for me to turn it off. The reason could not be identified

Rev. David Lee

at first, but now I know. In the book of Benny Hinn, he writes, "Use the music that has a human voice, do not use music that is only instrumental." The Holy Spirit says: "By all means, do not use music." It will go well with you to listen to the commands of the Holy Spirit.

3) Sprinkling the Blood of the Lord

If the secret place is prepared, it is a time to enter the tabernacle. There is a task that requires attention before opening the gates of the tabernacle, the sprinkling of Lord's blood.

The comparison between the sprinkled secret place and the secret place without the blood cannot be described in mere words. The difference is vast. As soon as entering the secret place, sprinkle all its sides. Sprinkle the walls, floors and even the ceilings. And begin to sprinkle on yourself. Proclaim these words as you sprinkle the blood of the Lord.

"I sprinkle the blood in the name of Jesus. The powers of all that are filthy and vile, be broken."

"I sprinkle the blood of the Lord. Be purified and made holy."

When the sprinkling of the blood is done on you, sprinkle until it begins to flow. Do not miss a spot from the head to toe. Be thorough. Although, the Holy Spirit has not spoken such instructions, I sprinkle three times on the head, face, shoulder, chest, stomach, reproductive organs and knees, in that order.

With an eager desire for a relationship with God, sprinkle the head. Sprinkle the face by looking up to the glory of God with a yearning heart. For the shoulder, ask for the authority of God to make a manifestation. Sprinkle on the chest, in requesting for the heart of God to be given you. The sprinkling of the stomach is to be done with a confession that all the filthy things of the world be cast out. For the reproductive organs, sprinkle with a petition, so that the lustful desires of the mind may be purified. Lastly, when sprinkling the knees, confess in the desire of health through the strengthening of the marrow, joints and bones.

Be seated as sprinkling is carried out. Do not kneel down. Take the position that is most comfortable for you. If the floor is too hard, grab a cushion or a blanket, so that you can be comfortable.

The reason behind this is to eliminate any misunderstandings caused by confusing the tabernacle effects as a result of a bodily discomfort. As one kneels down, the body is pressured down by the upper body weight, which can suppress the light sensations of the effect. It is necessary to pay attention in these areas, so that the tabernacle effects may not be distracted by the flesh, mind and the spirit.

The other important aspect is placing the hands facing upward. At first, I prayed many times by joining both hands together. But every time this was done, the Holy Spirit would say "Separate the hands. Face your palms upward." The necessity in doing so was not made clear, until the ministry invoked its importance. The reason in doing so was to feel the fire of the Holy Spirit and be able to sense even the lightest occurrences of the effects. Another reason behind the separation of hands is due to the difference in manifestations of the power from the right and the left. That is why the hands should not be joined.

And by sprinkling the blood in this manner, we are now ready to enter the gate of the tabernacle.

4) Gate of the Tabernacle and Jesus

The way to God is wide open. But the way to God can only be reached through Jesus.

"Jesus answered, 'I am the way and the truth and the life. No one comes to the Father except through me" (John 14:6)

Without entering through Jesus, no one can approach God. And to approach the Ark of the covenant, we must enter through the gate of the Tabernacle.

The gate of the tabernacle is made in four twisted linens. The linens used are blue, purple, scarlet and white. Many pastors describe these linens with a wide differing view, but the Holy Spirit has taught me the meaning behind each linen. I treasure more what the Holy Spirit has disclosed to me.

Blue represents Jesus as the life.
Purple represents Jesus as the King.
Scarlet represents the sufferings of Jesus.
White represents the resurrected Jesus.

The entering of the Gate of the tabernacle must be accompanied by confessions. These four missions of Jesus should come as a true confession from our heart. The confessions can be made inwardly or outwardly through speaking. Also the confessions stated above can be made longer through its added confessions. For example, "Jesus, our life, I will be fruitful and increase in number on this earth." Or "King Jesus, Lord, I serve you as my King, as your people, I serve." "Jesus, as you suffered for my sake, I will suffer like you in living for others." "Resurrected

Jesus, as you broke the chains of death in resurrection. I will likewise overcome these problems and live a victorious life." Any methods of confessions like these are good.

Now, if the confessions are made, the permission has been granted for you to open the gates of the Tabernacle.

5) Death at the Altar of Burnt Offering

After opening the gate, the first thing that comes into sight is the altar of burnt offering. Fire is already burning at the altar of burnt offering. A slain animal is laid at the altar of burnt offering. And as all is consumed, only ashes remain.

Now it is your turn. Climb up the altar of burnt offering by your own effort. Climb and take a stand on the altar of burnt offering. Feel the fire burning. This fire is not of this world. This isn't some fire from a stove, or made with gas. It is the Fire of God. This fire has been kindled by God.

The fire of God consumes you. As the fire of God begins to consume you, ask for your ego to be burned. Burn the ego that once professed yourself as best. And burn that self confidence. As you burn the flesh and mind, then you will begin to sense the spirit reviving. Take a look at those ashes that once was your flesh and mind. Feel your spirit that has been set free from the flesh and mind.

And, in this way, you can come down from the altar of burnt offering.

6) Repentance at the Wash Basin

Repentance has to be made at the wash basin. The repentance must be honest. Without possessing a sense of having been a sinner, you cannot enter into the holy place. You must be purified. Purification is linked closely concerning the flesh.

Try to be fervent when repenting. Try your best to pour out your heart. Make a loud noise. Wail with all your heart until your eyes begin to shed tears and your nose runs. Stronger repentance results in the deeper manifestation of God's glory.

7) Petition and Declaration at the Bread of Presence

When the repentance is made, we gain an approval to enter the holy place. The holy place also has an entrance. Open the door and enter through it. Then, on the right side will be laid, the bread of presence, the left side with the golden lamp stand and the altar of incense. All these will be located in front of the most holy place.

Take the time to make a petition at the bread of presence. If possible, make the petition in detail. It is very wrong to think that, because God knows everything. We do not need to speak of these things. God already knows what your prayers are concerned about. But what God wants from you is to make a petition and without a petition, God will ignore the prayer. Make a note of this. Make your petitions as detailed as possible. For example, request the exact amount of money that is needed. Describe the pain in detail. That is how a petition is made that will bring you an answer.

If the petition has been made, begin to make a declaration in relation to the petitions. Yes, the declarations can be made after each petition, or can be bundled into one declaration after the petition has been made. The important aspect is: 'petition - declaration – thanksgiving' should all be made as a single bundle.

When the declaration is made, speak in such a way "In the name of Jesus the Nazarene, all the cancer cell replication, stop! And be destroyed at this very hour." Repeat it 3 times in a row. While the declaration is being made without ceasing 3 times, plan ahead on what should be said next. Make the declaration specific. For example, "In the name of Jesus the Nazarene, my bank account should be filled with $500 dollars now,".

When the declaration has been made, lift up your thanksgiving in response to those declarations. "My father God, I thank you that the cancer cells within me have been destroyed completely." "My father God, I thank you that $500 has been placed in my bank account." Remember, the prayer of thanksgiving is a prayer of faith. It is not about praying what will be obtained. It is about giving thanks concerning the things that have already been given. A prayer concerning the things to be obtained is 'hope,' but the prayer concerning the things already given is 'faith'.

8) Welcoming the Holy Spirit at Golden Lamp Stand

If the petition, declaration and thanksgiving have been lifted up, take the time and invite the Holy Spirit at the golden lamp stand. If the prayer until now has been concerned about the prayers of flesh and mind, now it is about connecting the prayer of the mind to the prayer of the spirit.

Without the help of the Holy Spirit, it is impossible to experience the glory of God. That is why inviting the Holy Spirit is very important.

Confess in such a way. "Holy Spirit, I invite you at this very hour. Be with me Holy Spirit so that I may experience the glory of God. Guide me." "Holy Spirit, I commit to you this very hour."

"Holy Spirit, I serve you at this hour." "I delight and welcome you this hour, Holy Spirit. Thank you for giving me this moment." There may be other aspects not mentioned here, so invite the Holy Spirit as the heart is being reminded. With it, the Holy Spirit will begin to guide you to the Ark of the Covenant.

9) Prayer in Tongues at the Altar of Incense

When the welcoming process of inviting the Holy Spirit is done, begin to pray in tongues at the golden lamp stand. Try to pray in tongues with speed, loudness, power and in a higher tone. Do it with an utmost sincerity and with a fervent heart.

Do not try to translate the tongues being spoken. The importance does not lie in your ability to translate the tongues. The utmost importance is in being able to experience the mighty glory of God in this hour. So do not translate, but concentrate on being active in the spirit.

Do not think of other things. Some meditate on a pot placed on a stove while praying in tongues, please do not do these things. As more useless thoughts begin to occur, pray in tongues with a louder voice and more power. As this progresses on, suddenly you will feel the spirit starting to become active, and you will begin to witness 'you,' being already inside the most holy place.

10) Being still at the Most Holy Place

When the prayer in tongues ends, begin to praise in tongues. Do not contemplate on what song should be picked. This praise is not on your lips. Of course, the prayer leader must sing the praise through the lips. But when praying by your self, do not involve praising with the lips. Only praise through the spirit. When you praise through the spirit, a natural understanding of the praise in tongues will occur. A pitch of a song that had never been heard will be heard. Even the praises of angels will be heard.

Praise by following along with that music. Incline your ear to the sound of praise and begin to follow by slowly praising in the spirit. This is the real praise. It is wonderful. The praise of the angels is beautiful. As you praise along, if possible, try to record it on your phone. This praise is the very praise of the heavens and is exceedingly precious.

As the praise of the spirit is being carried along, you can feel yourself already being inside the most holy place. Now, you must not move. Not even your fingers. Do not move your eyebrows; do not swallow your saliva. As if paralyzed, stay still. Even if a fly lands on you, do not drive it away. Just experience the glory together.

Demons will bother your flesh in this very hour. That is why your body itches or bothers you, especially at this hour. If you move in this moment, everything goes for nothing. Do not make a movement, but only let your spirit be active in this moment.

If you are listening to the voice of the Holy Spirit, follow his instructions. The Holy Spirit will ask you "What do you see?" Then look, and something will become visible. Do not reply back to the Holy Spirit as "I see something" by speaking out loud. Do not speak. Continue to talk to the Holy Spirit as he leads you, follow him. By doing so, one is able to arrive at the atonement cover and the Ark of the Covenant.

11) Experience God's Glory at the Ark of the Covenant.

The Holy Spirit will require you to sprinkle the blood of Jesus once again. Whoever is not able to hear the voice of the Holy Spirit should imagine himself standing in front of the atonement cover followed by the sprinkling of Jesus' blood. Remember to sprinkle it in the spirit, not with the hands. Take this to your heart. Your flesh and mind are dead, they do not exist. Moving your mouth and hands is a pointless prayer. Is anyone still making movements with the hands? Do not do this.

Entering the Ark of the Covenant happens after having passed through the atonement cover. It is not possible to enter into the Ark of the Covenant. Ark of the Covenant is 2.5 cubits X 1.5 Cubits X 1.5 Cubits. It is very small in size. That is why entering the Ark of the Covenant is primarily symbolic. You do not actually enter into the Ark of the Covenant, but rather your spirit imagines the Ark of the Covenant as you experience the glory of God.

After having passed through the atonement cover, consider all places as the Ark of the Covenant. The Ark of the Covenant is not a small box, but a place that contains an enormous world. At this place, we can meet, talk and hug the Lord. The Lord can take us to the beach or even visit the heavens together. The Lord can scoop up the living water for us to drink and tell us the secret things of heaven. We can find out the things that others struggle with, by talking to the Lord and we can even make an intercessory prayer through this information.

When we are talking and being together with the Lord, the Holy Spirit awaits in stillness. You will begin to realize that the Lord and the Holy Spirit are different entities. The Holy Spirit is the counselor, who is with us on this earth, but you will realize that God, Jesus and Holy Spirit exist in different entities. This truth is very simple and easy to understand but many people in the world do not try to understand it. They prefer to wait in preparation to speak against those who make such claims.

Keep in mind that the Holy Spirit has led you to the Ark of the Covenant. Without the Lord, we cannot approach God, and without the Holy Spirit, we cannot approach the Lord.

"As it is written: No eye has seen, no ear has heard, no mind has conceived what God has prepared for those who love him, but God has revealed it to us by his spirit. The spirit searches all things, even the deep things of God. For who among men knows the thoughts of a man except the man's spirit within him? In the same way no one knows the thoughts of God except the spirit of God." (1 Corinthians 2:9-11)

The Holy Spirit is the spirit of God. The realm of God can only be revealed through the Holy Spirit. Keeping a close relationship with the Holy Spirit is the only way to obtain the secrets of heaven. Did you talk to the Holy Spirit? Congratulations. Did you meet the Lord? Congratulations to you.

Do not delight in the simple notion of having achieved such a feat. Rather be thankful to the Holy Spirit, who has caused you to meet the Lord through his unfathomable love. The Holy Spirit will continue to lead you in that way until the day you enter into Heaven. Hallelujah!

4. Glory of God

1) Light of God

To focus on God means to entering into the glory of God. The glory of God resides in the center of the light. The light is the direct opposite of darkness, and God is light. Jesus came into the world as the light of the world. But the darkness has not understood the coming of the light.

"In him was life, and that life was the light of men. The light shines in the darkness, but the darkness has not understood it" (John 1:4-5).

Anything that interferes with focusing on God is darkness. However small the candle light might be, the light drives away the darkness by shining in the midst of it. These are the characteristics of light and darkness. The person remaining in the light does not reside in darkness.

The Bible speaks in this way, "For God, who said, "Let light shine out of darkness," made his light shine in our hearts to give us the light of the knowledge of the glory of God in the face of Christ." (2 Corinthians 4:6). The glorious light of God is already shining down upon our hearts. When the light is received in full measure and is used, the darkness is cast away.

The Bible also says, "Arise, shine, for your light has come, and the glory of the LORD rises upon you" (Isaiah 60:1). This is to say that the glory of God, the light of Jesus, has shined on us; we are to take the stand in reflecting back the light. This is not a choice but a command of God. The light has been made manifest in you, now stand and shine the light. In so doing, the darkness of the world will be purged and all that will remain is the glory of God.

But many saints do not understand this light and can't use the light. How lamentable is this. We do not even understand that God has already given us his glorious light, but the truth is not accepted and we lack the desire to obtain this light. How sorrowful can this be? It is as stated, "This is the verdict: Light has come into the world, but men loved darkness instead of light, because their deeds were evil." (John 3:19). The glory of God ultimately can be experienced by understanding and living in the light of Christ.

2) Glory of God

Experiencing God's glory is to be shined on by the light of God. This light is an understanding from God.

Ezekiel witnessed that the glory of God shined.

"I saw the glory of the God of Israel coming from the east. His voice was like the roar of rushing waters, and the land was radiant with his glory" (Ezekiel 43:2).

The Apostle John was lifted by the Holy Spirit to witness the glory of God, in which, the place was filled with lights.

"It shone with the glory of God, and its brilliance was like that of a very precious jewel, like a jasper, clear as crystal" (Revelations 21:11).

"The city does not need the sun or the moon to shine on it, for the glory of God gives it light, and the lamb is its lamp" (Revelations 21:23).

From God's view, it is a light, but in the eyes of men, it is a fire. The Bible records, "To the Israelites the glory of the LORD looked like a consuming fire on top of the mountain" (Exodus 24:17). When the glory of God descended upon the mountain, people felt the glory like that of a fire. Therefore, the glory of God is about receiving the fire. The fundamental understanding is the same in its glory, light and fire.

The light is that of Christ's light and the glory of God is the fire of the Holy Spirit. The Bible points to Jesus as, "The Son is the radiance of God's glory and the exact representation of his being," (Hebrews 1:3). Jesus is the radiance of God's glory. The glory of God shines as the light shines through Jesus. That is why the light, glory and fire share the same meaning.

3) God

Who do you worship? Is it God? Or is it the world? A person belonging to flesh will serve the world. But the person belonging to the spirit will serve God.

Jesus spoke to the Samaritan woman, "Yet a time is coming, and has now come, when the true worshipers will worship the Father in the spirit and truth, for they are the kind of worshipers the Father seeks" (John 4:23).

Jesus says that, "God is the spirit, and his worshipers must worship in the spirit and in truth" (John 4:24).

Many will think from this verse that God only resides in a spirit form. But God far surpasses a simple spiritual being.

Identifying God as a formless spirit that does not take shape or form is a very dangerous idea. Apostle John on the isle of Patmos saw the form of God through the Holy Spirit, and described it in the following way:

"At once I was in the spirit, and there before me was a throne in heaven with someone sitting on it. And the one who sat there had the appearance of jasper and carnelian. A rainbow, resembling an emerald, encircled the throne" (Revelations 4:2-3).

'The Throne in heaven with someone sitting on it' points to God. The Apostle John clearly states that he has witnessed the appearance of God. The appearance of God was said to be encircled by jasper, carnelian and a rainbow. This goes on to say that the glory of God is great and mighty.

Apostle John is not the only person to have seen the appearance of God. Moses also saw the appearance of God. Moses in his written text describes the scene.

"Moses and Aaron, Nadab and Abihu, and the seventy elders of Israel went up and saw the God of Israel. Under his feet was something like a pavement made of sapphire, clear as the sky itself. But God did not raise his hand against these leaders of the Israelites; they saw God, and they ate and drank" (Exodus 24:9-11).

Moses with Aaron, Nadab, Abihu and the seventy Elders of Israel together saw God. They all saw God, and ate and drank under the feet of God. Moses actually saw the back of God.

"Then I will remove my hand and you will see my back; but my face must not be seen" (Exodus 33:23).

There is another person who has seen the appearance of God. That is the priest Ezekiel. Ezekiel goes on to describe God in the following way:

"Above the expanse over their heads was what looked like a throne of sapphire, and high above on the throne was a figure like that of a man. I saw that from what appeared to be his waist up he looked like glowing metal, as if full of fire, and that from there down he looked like fire; and brilliant light surrounded him. Like the appearance of a rainbow in the clouds on a rainy day, so was the radiance around him. This was the appearance of the likeness of the glory of the LORD. When I saw it, I fell facedown, and I heard the voice of one speaking" (Ezekiel 1:26-28).

Ezekiel describes the appearance of God as "like that of a man." He saw God and above and below the waist area of God.

Do not think that it's odd to have described God's appearance in such a plain way. Isn't it more odd to think that the God we serve is nothing but a formless spiritual being? How can one claim to know God without even knowing the appearance of God, whom we serve?

4) What God Wants

Just like the other normal days, I began to open the gates of the prayer. As always, the blood of Jesus was sprinkled all around the place and on myself as well. Then I proceeded to sit down.

As I mentioned earlier, I pray in the order of the prayer of flesh, prayer of the mind and prayer of the spirit. As the prayer of the flesh would wind down, the prayer of the mind would begin, and as it finished, I would pray the prayer of the spirit. And as always has been the voice of the Holy Spirit spoke and asked this question of me.

"David, what do you believe the glory of God is?"

"... ... ..."

"The glory of God is you."

The Holy Spirit seemed to have read my mind, and he began to explain further. Then, he asked liked this:

"David, do you know when God is most delighted?"

I had figured that the answer to the Holy Spirit's question had been perfectly understood in my mind. It is not a tough thing to know that God delights the most in a faithful and diligent lifestyle, that strives for the kingdom of God and his righteousness. So I rushed in, giving my reply to him.

"I believe that it is about building a big church through hard work for God ......"

What I really wanted was to reply with 'striving with a great effort in ministry for the kingdom of God and his righteousness,' but without knowing, building a 'big church' was spoken out loud. My secret of the heart was revealed. With the mouth, 'striving for the kingdom of God and his righteousness' was spoken, but deep within my heart, I must have yearned for building a big church.

"David, what God wants is just 'you'."

To the core, the words of the Holy Spirit had shaken my entire being. I almost passed out. It was too surprising. What God wanted was no other thing but 'me'. That truth was simply amazing.

The Holy Spirit added more to his words, as I could not refrain from the amazement.

"David, God is not interested in your ministry. He is most delighted when he has just 'you.'"

Saying that, the Holy Spirit made me recall the words of Zephaniah chapter 3 verse 17, which I remembered.

"The LORD your God is with you, he is mighty to save. He will take great delight in you, he will quiet you with his love, he will rejoice over you with singing" (Zephaniah 3:17).

God was a God who delights in looking upon me. I did not know this truth and had been wandering aimlessly for the things that God might be delighted in. The reality was that God delighted in seeing me, but I had been trying hard to make God happy by doing other things.

God explained that I was the Glory of God. It is not because I am special that God makes me to be his glory. It is not dependent on my ability or in the success of ministries that makes me the glory of God. It is simply God as a father, glorifying his sons and daughters. This is just like the parents who think proudly of their sons and daughters. As a parent, we always think of our sons and daughters proudly. There is a no parent who would be ashamed or think less of their offspring. Even though a child may leave a wound in their hearts, that child is still a glorious being to the parents. In the proverbs of Korea, "There is not a finger that does not hurt after biting down on all 10 fingers," as such the heart of parents are all similar.

A child that parents worry about is an immature child. This reminds me of Pastor David Younggi Cho's sermon. It was during a cold winter, when Pastor Cho was ministering in a tent church.

Without missing a single day, an elderly lady and Pastor Cho always prayed an all night prayer. Pastor Cho appreciated the elderly lady, but his heart ached as he considered the well being of the elderly lady. And as the morning would approach, the elderly lady's daughter-in-law would always bring a well brewed coffee. As if coming from a wealthy family, the daughter in law's clothing made an impression. It triggered his curiosity, and in consideration of this odd situation, he asked the elderly lady.

"Lady, from what it appears, your daughter-in-law seems to be well off. Why don't you stay with her in a warm room ... rather than spend all night in a tent during such a cold weather?"

To Pastor Cho, the words of the elderly lady have remained with him for life.

The elderly lady replied to Pastor Cho like this.

"Pastor, I have three boys. The first and the second son are living a good life, but the last one is not doing so well. How can I as a mother sleep in comfort, when my last son is not living so well?"

Regarding us, God's heart is no different than that of the elderly lady. As the heart of parents lean towards a child who is worrisome, the heart of God dwells upon the weak child. After having found out that the sole interest of God is in 'me,' my attitude towards the church ministry changed completely. How many of us focus on things other than 'me,' when the interest of God is 'me'? As the interest of God is in 'me,' our interests must be 'God'. This is the way it should be, and it is the right order of things.

Even after this conversation, the Holy Spirit continued to explain many times about the glory of God. The Holy Spirit revealed another aspect concerning the Glory of God.

The prophet Habakkuk wrote the revelation received from God in this way:

"For the earth will be filled with the knowledge of the glory of the LORD, as the waters cover the sea" (Habakkuk 2:14)

The framework of this text is written in a contrast format. The 'water and sea' is placed in contrast with the 'glory and earth'. But the prophet Habakkuk utilizes this contrast in a slightly uncertain way. If written in a proper contrast format, the verse would appear to be like this.

"As the water covers the sea, the glory of the Lord will fill the earth'.

But with a deeper observation, the verse states, "For the earth will be filled with the knowledge of the glory of the Lord." Why did prophet Habakkuk write in such a way? The Holy Spirit gave an answer to my curiosity.

"David. The glory of the Lord has already filled the earth. As the water covers the sea, the glory of the Lord is already covering the earth."

A new understanding of God's glory began to fall upon my heart. Until now, I had been trying to pass on the glory of the Lord. In a spiritual training, I insisted on passing the glory of God to the people of the earth. But what the Holy Spirit spoke has changed my paradigm in understanding the glory of God completely.

I had not realized the truth of God's glory, already covering the entire earth. What God wanted was to have the people of this earth affirm the glory of the Lord. The glory of the Lord already being upon the earth, and its people not affirming that glory, was understood in that moment of truth.

This word also applies to a hard working and religious believer. In comparison to the earthly, the church is more filled with the glory of God, but how many people still do not experience the glory of God?

5) Differing Glories

Acknowledging the glory of God can not be achieved in a single day. After all, the experiences of God's glory widely differ from person to person in its depth and width. This goes on to say that each experience differs with each person. Paul describes in a following manner.

"There are also heavenly bodies and there are earthly bodies; but the splendor of the heavenly bodies is one kind, and the splendor of the earthly bodies is another. The sun has one kind of splendor, the moon another and the stars another ; and star differs from star in splendor" (1 Corinthians 15:40-41).

The Glory of God is not simple. Maybe for an individual it may be simple. It is because that person is receiving a satisfactory glory of God on him or her self. But the Glory of God cannot be described in its full measure in that way. The glory of God differs from one person to another. Paul explains this aspect. Some are satisfied with the glories of the earth, but the other person is satisfied only with the glories of heaven. That is a glory, when this also is a glory. But there are clear differences in these types of glories.

A person of the flesh lives by the glories of the earth, but the spiritual person lives through the glory of God. As the sun, moon and stars all differ in their light, the glories of God also differ.

As one star's light differs from the other star, so is the glory of God that differs. We must experience the higher glory of God. This is as if one glory is placed upon another glory. His glory has no end. Until the age of death is reached, our experience of God's glory must continue and reach a higher level. As you begin to experience the deeper glory of God, the abilities in you will begin to grow mightily. But this special privilege is only granted to those who are experiencing the glory of God. The person who has not even once experienced the glory of God will not be able to build one glory upon another.

The kingdom of God is always the same. Whoever possesses more of the kingdom of God will gain more. But whoever does not have the kingdom of God will never have it and the one who does not put his talent to use, even what he has will be taken away. The kingdom of God always pours more grace upon those who experience grace and more power is given to those with power.

6) Pillar of Fire and Pillar of Cloud

The best way to describe the glory of God, light of Christ, and fire of the Holy Spirit is by entering through the tabernacle. That is why an understanding of the Tabernacle is very important. Can you recall the 'pillar of fire'?

When leaving the land of Egypt, the people of Israel were led by the pillar of fire and the pillar of cloud. The Israelites always saw and walked with the pillars of fire and cloud.

"And they will tell the inhabitants of this land about it. They have already heard that you, O LORD, are with these people and that you, O LORD, have been seen face to face, that your cloud stays over them, and that you go before them in a pillar of cloud by day and a pillar of fire by night" (Numbers 14:14).

This pillar of fire represents the guidance of God. The Israelites constructed the tabernacle in the middle of the camp. The twelve tribes were divided in the groups of three on each side of the tabernacle. When the tabernacle moved, the Israelites also moved. The Israelites followed wherever the tabernacle led. If the tabernacle settled, its people also settled there. This did not matter if it settled for days or many months. The movement was determined by following the tabernacle.

The pillar of cloud and fire always stayed on the tabernacle. The lifting of the pillar of cloud from the tabernacle meant a signal. Whenever the pillar of cloud was lifted, the Levites would pack up the tabernacle and follow wherever the pillar of fire led them.

"In all the travels of the Israelites, whenever the cloud lifted from above the tabernacle, they would set out; but if the cloud did not lift, they did not set out--until the day it lifted" (Exodus 40:36-37).

The pillar of fire and the cloud stayed side by side in the time of night and morning in leading the Israelites. It is not true that the pillar of Fire only led during the night time and the pillar of Cloud led only in the morning. There were times when both pillars accompanied each other.

7) The Two Pillars at the Red Sea

When the Israelites left Egypt and were confronted at the Red Sea, the Chariots and armies of Egypt were in a close pursuit of the Israelites. The heart of the Pharaoh was hardened again. The people of Israel felt an imminent danger upon them. But God commanded Moses to divide the Red Sea so that the Israelites could cross the divided sea. The number of Israelites amounted to approximately 2 million to 3 million. Even if the people walked through the sea in a haste, that many people cannot cross within a mere 1 hour to 2 hours. Those people crossed the sea through the entire night.

In this suspenseful moment, an amazing event occurs. The Bible records that the angel of God led the people of Israel in the front. The pillar of cloud was with the angel of God. Then, the pillar of cloud moved to the rear of the Israelites. This is the pillar that moved between the Israelites and the Egyptian army. The Bible describes the scene in this way.

"Then the angel of God, who had been traveling in front of Israel's army, withdrew and went behind them. The pillar of cloud also moved from in front and stood behind them, coming between the armies of Egypt and Israel. Throughout the night the cloud brought darkness to the one side and light to the other side; so neither went near the other all night long" (Exodus 14:19-20).

What phenomenon happened when the pillar of cloud intervened in between the Israelites and the Egyptian army? Isn't it recorded that the side of the Egyptian armies were in darkness but the side of the Israelites had light. Can you grasp what this is saying? The pillar of cloud separated the Egyptian army and the Israelites, and the Pillar of fire shined upon the Israelites. Why did the pillar of fire shine upon the Israelites throughout the night? The Israelites needed light in order to cross the sea. Without it, it would have been difficult to cross the sea.

It was the working of the pillar of fire and pillar of cloud together. The Bible states, "During the last watch of the night the LORD looked down from the pillar of fire and cloud at the Egyptian army and threw it into confusion" (Exodus 14:24). The gathering of the Pillar of fire and cloud happened at night, and is known to have been together until the early morning.

As such, the pillar of fire and cloud worked together. Even though the appearance of fire and cloud differ, in representation of God's glory, they are working in conjunction with each other. If the pillar of fire was used to reveal the glory of God, so was the pillar of cloud. Moses recorded that the tabernacle was so filled with the cloud that he could not approach the tent of meeting.

"Moses could not enter the tent of meeting because the cloud had settled upon it, and the glory of the LORD filled the tabernacle" (Exodus 40:35).

The cloud was the glory of God. Moses could not approach the tent of meeting because it was filled with the cloud. Actually, the cloud of God covered the tent of meting. But that day, the cloud had entered into the tent of meeting in a full measure.

The glory of God descending in a cloud did not only happen during the time of Moses. When the temple of Solomon was completed, a similar phenomenon occurred. Solomon could no longer worship, due to the cloud.

"So that the priests could not stand to minister because of the cloud, for the glory of the Lord filled the house of the Lord" (1 Kings 8:11).

As told, the cloud is the actual presence of God's glory. The cloud of God is sovereign and the authority is so holy that no one was able to approach, or even withstand, its mighty power.

Ezekiel experienced a similar occurrence. As the presence of God descended, the temple began to fill with a cloud.

"Then the glory of the LORD rose from above the cherubim and moved to the threshold of the temple. The cloud filled the temple, and the court was full of the radiance of the glory of the LORD" (Ezekiel 10:4).

The cloud that represents the glory of God always remained upon the tabernacle. The cloud of God did not reside only in the light of day. Even at night, the pillar of cloud remained.

"So the cloud of the LORD was over the tabernacle by day, and fire was in the cloud by night, in the sight of all the house of Israel during all their travel" (Exodus 40:38).

This verse shows the pillar of fire remaining in the middle of the pillar of cloud. Can you see, as the pillar of cloud covered the tabernacle, the pillar of fire always remained on the Tent of Meeting? The pillar of fire and cloud are not something that appears and disappears or ceases to exist. As the glory of God is eternal, so are the pillar of fire and cloud. Isn't it only right that as the pillar of cloud remained on the Tent of Meeting, the pillar of fire would always remain upon the most holy place?

5. Way of meeting the Holy Spirit

You may already possess the gift in hearing the voice of the Holy Spirit. You may even have the ability in seeing visions and have various other gifts. It is such a commendable and respectable thing in being able to see visions, hear and possess gifts of the Holy Spirit. And many people may regard you with honor and respect, in following you.

Many seek the spiritual gifts. And many go in search for those who are a minister of power. They follow any famous person. Even visit many prayer houses. It is because they want to receive the spiritual gifts. We always envy those who possess the gifts of the spirit. By comparing ourselves with those who possess more gifts, we make ourselves out to be smaller.

Many people go on seeking for the spiritual gifts, but only a handful receive the gifts. This is why it's so easy to slip into 'Pride' for those who possess the spiritual gifts. And that 'pride' is quick to destroy that person.

1) The Holy Spirit and Gifts

Everyone desires to have the spiritual gifts. The reason may be that the way of receiving the Holy Spirit has been made available to anyone. In the age of the Old Testament, only the chosen ones were able to receive the gifts of the spirit. The gifts were usually given to the prophets or seers. Therefore, common people did not even dream of receiving the gifts of the spirit. However, as Jesus came to this earth, he often spoke of the 'Holy Spirit'. As he was ascending to the heaven, a command to wait on the Holy Spirit was spoken. And like the words of Jesus, the Holy Spirit was made manifest to many people within just a few days.

The book of Acts, chapter 2 talks about the manifestation of the Holy Spirit like that of a wind and fire.

"When the day of Pentecost came, they were all together in one place. Suddenly a sound like the blowing of a violent wind came from heaven and filled the whole house where they were sitting. They saw what seemed to be tongues of fire that separated and came to rest on each of them. All of them were filled with the Holy Spirit and began to speak in other tongues as the spirit enabled them" (Acts 2:1-4).

The people at that time, who received the power of the Holy Spirit, were not a special group of people. Yes, they did gather at Mark's upper room by risking their own lives as a small group of people professing Jesus, but they weren't prophets or a seer. They were just a common group of people, but the Holy Spirit manifested to those gathered in that place. Isn't this amazing?

Though, in the time of the Old Testament, the Holy Spirit did manifest itself to certain individuals, resulting in the power of the gift. There was a time when the Holy Spirit manifested itself to King Saul, who did not know anything but war.

"When they arrived at Gibeah, a procession of prophets met him; the spirit of God came upon him in power, and he joined in their prophesying" (1 Samuel 10:10).

At that time, King Saul was obsessed with killing David, who had not sinned against him. He wanted to kill David by any means necessary, thinking that his throne would be made secure with it.

There was not an occurrence when the Holy Spirit's power manifested itself to many people at once, like in the book of Acts chapter 2. Yes, there was a time when the Holy Spirit led the entire nation of people into a repentance, and fought on many battlefields through the power of the Holy Spirit. But most of the Holy Spirit's workings were done through one certain leader, not with everyone all at once. Moreover, the manifestation of the Holy Spirit's power to each individual, as the ministers of the spirit, is a surprising phenomenon.

2) Powers of the Holy Spirit

When the powers of the Holy Spirit, manifested at the upper room of Mark, the 120 saints in the room began to act with great power. The book of Acts describes in detail, of powers given to them.

Peter is the first person to be mentioned. As we all know, Peter was a man who was as common as anyone gets. He was a fisherman without having gone through any form of education. On top of this, Peter is known for his cowardly act in denying Jesus three times as Jesus was taken to the house of the high priest in the hands of the soldiers. But, this same Peter became bold as to speak out loudly concerning Jesus.

"Then Peter stood up with the eleven, raised his voice and addressed the crowd: "Fellow Jews and all of you who live in Jerusalem, let me explain this to you; listen carefully to what I say" (Acts 2:14).

What was the scene like? The land of Israel was at the beginning of Pentecost. Every year, when Pentecost would begin, Jews scattered throughout all the nations would come back to their home land to worship. Just as the people of Korea are scattered throughout the nations now, the Jews were also living in many different nations. The scattered people would worship the local synagogues, but in these times of national celebration, the people would go back to their homeland with the purpose of worshiping at the temple.

Peter began preaching in a 'raised voice' to these crowds of people. The sermon of Peter at that place cannot be recorded in its full measure, but the purpose of the delivery was on 'Jesus'. The truth of Jesus, who is the son of God and the savior of the world was told, in that he was killed by the hands of the people.

This type of sermon could have resulted in another crucifixion. Peter could have died like Jesus on the cross, because of this sermon. The background of this historic period revolved around Christians hiding from the high priests and the soldiers, so that Christians could worship in secret. Anyone caught would be exiled from the community of Jews and in the worst case, could result in crucifixion. But surprisingly, the response of the people differed than in the time of Jesus. With the words of Peter, people were cut to the heart with guilt, and they began to repent.

"When the people heard this, they were cut to the heart and said to Peter and the other apostles, "brothers, what shall we do?" (Acts 2:37).

This is an amazing scene. Isn't this the working of the Holy Spirit's power? To explain, it is not because of the words of Peter, but by the Holy Spirit speaking through the lips of Peter that the heart of the crowd was captivated. The number of people who repented when received forgiveness of sins through the sermon of Peter, was 3,000. Isn't it incredible? Through a single sermon, its hearers numbering thousands were transformed into the people of God. Maybe there are some who would view with skepticism, "Doubt it ... isn't it only possible because it was in the era of Acts? Would such a thing happen now?" Yes, workings greater than that of Peter are happening now. A German minster of the spirit, named Reinhart Bonnke is calling thousands upon thousands of people in repentance through a gathering. An average number of 2,000,000 people gather at a single event. Each are given a flyer as an encouragement in leaving with a commitment of conviction. And simply by stirring the hearts, each event would still record thousands upon thousands of commitments. And the participants are Muslims. Hallelujah!

It is not only Peter who was able to undertake such a task. The story of Stephen comes up in Acts Chapter 6. Stephen was not one of the twelve, but he was chosen to serve the early church. The Holy Spirit manifested mightily through Stephen.

"Now Stephen, a man full of God's grace and power, did great wonders and miraculous signs among the people. Opposition arose, however, from members of the Synagogue of the Freedmen (as it was called)--Jews of Cyrene and Alexandria as well as the provinces of Cilicia and Asia. These men began to argue with Stephen, but they could not stand up against his wisdom or the spirit by whom he spoke" (Acts 6:8-10).

Stephen did great wonders and miraculous signs when the grace and power of the Holy Spirit manifested itself in full measure. Not one person was able to overcome Stephen in arguing. The power of the Holy Spirit had given Stephen a surpassing wisdom over the others. deacon Philip's story follows after the story of Stephen.

"Philip went down to a city in Samaria and proclaimed the Christ there. When the crowds heard Philip and saw the miraculous signs he did, they all paid close attention to what he said. With shrieks, evil spirits came out of many, and many paralytics and cripples were healed. So there was great joy in that city" (Acts 8:5-8).

Philip focused on delivering the message of Jesus to the Samaritans whom the Jews shunned. The signs of miracles and wonders were done at the city of Samaria. The spirits were cast out, the oppressed were set free from their paralysis, and the lame were made well. The great joy in the city of Samaria came about through Philip.

Likewise, the disciples who received the power of the Holy Spirit spread throughout the region performing great signs and miracles. This gospel in a short span had spread throughout the entire world in the year 313 A.D, the Emperor Constantine proclaimed Christianity to be the Rome's national religion.

This was only possible through the working of the Holy Spirit. The people, enraptured by this power of the Holy Spirit, did not neglect anyone in being rich or poor, but focused on spreading the gospel. The wonders were not differentiated based upon being male or female. The people oppressed by the demons and drunk from the lust of this world were set free. They were set free in the spirit of the Lord, and this freedom was enough to change the nation of Rome. The emperor of Rome had to make Christianity the national religion and Christianity began to spread throughout the world.

Even now, so many miracles, signs and wonders are done among the ministers of the spirit. The dead are raised, and yes, the lame are made well, the blind can see again, and the deaf can hear. All these miracles are happening now. Is this it? The gold sprinkles come down from the heaven and people without money to treat their teeth are experiencing miracles and develop a golden tooth. All these miracles are possible only by the power of the Holy Spirit. Our Lord also received the Holy Spirit's power in conducting his ministries. Luke, in his writing, describes as follows:

"How God anointed Jesus of Nazareth with the Holy Spirit and power, and how he went around doing good and healing all who were under the power of the devil, because God was with him" (Acts 10:38).

As the Lord ministered through the manifestation of the Holy Spirit, the ministers of the spirit on this earth are ministering only by the receiving of the Holy Spirit's power. They are not doing it on their own. These things are only possible through the power of the Holy Spirit. Hallelujah!

3) The Holy Spirit, whom I have to meet

Power of the Holy Spirit is owned by the Holy Spirit. That is why the power of the Holy Spirit is held by the Holy Spirit. Even though the manifestation of the Holy Spirit may work through a person, that manifestation of power is the Holy Spirit. Many overlook this truth. Why are you so persistent in following that person, if the signs, wonders and miracles are centralized in the Holy Spirit? What is it about that person that you get so attached to? That person has the workings of the Holy Spirit? Yes. What you have said is completely right. Indeed, that person does possess the power of the Holy Spirit. Then, who is the Holy Spirit that is in you? Is the Holy Spirit, who manifests itself in that person the only real one, and thereby says that you have the fake Holy Spirit? Where is your capability to reason?

The Holy Spirit in you is 100% God, and the Holy Spirit in that person whom you follow is also 100% Holy Spirit. It is not that the other person's Holy Spirit is more powerful. The Holy Spirit in that person and in you are both the same Holy Spirit. It is not by looking at the other person's Holy Spirit that you are able to recognize the Holy Spirit in you. Leave the other person alone so that he may be consumed by the Holy Spirit. You are meant to enjoy the Holy Spirit in you.

Do you know why God hates adultery the most? The reason lies within its 'worshiping of idols'. Having an intimate relationship with your spouse is not termed as adultery. What we call adultery is sharing an intimate relationship with someone other than your spouse. 'The worship of idols' is adultery to God. That is why God tells his people to not commit adultery. Committing adultery hurts the heart of the spouse, but at the same time it leaves a scar on the heart of God. It may be arguable that the death of a spouse causes greater stress, but in some aspect it may be the adultery that causes greater stress. This is the greatest betrayal and an unbearable pain.

Longing and desiring after the Holy Spirit in others is like committing adultery. This is a betrayal and a disgrace to the Holy Spirit who walks with me. It ignores and betrays the Holy Spirit who is with me. "Pastor, it is simply because ... I cannot feel that the Holy Spirit is with me... that is why." Don't make such a statement. Have you tried really hard? Have you really desired the Holy Spirit, to be with you? Were there ever times of solitude spent with the Holy Spirit? Just because you can't feel him, don't go looking for the Holy Spirit in others. Just because you haven't discovered the Holy Spirit in yourself, it doesn't mean he doesn't exist.

4) The first path in meeting with the Holy Spirit

How did you get to know the Holy Spirit? How do you walk with the Holy Spirit? I am well acquainted in the ways of walking with the Holy Spirit. These are not proud words. I have come to experience many things through the length of time spent in walking with the Holy Spirit. The Holy Spirit has taught me many lessons in walking with him.

In my case, I first needed the 'desire'. Perhaps, this is required of everyone. 'To desire' is very important. When there is a desire, we are interested and are able to devote time to it. This desire results in seeking out a 'secret place' to be alone. Occasionally, there are some who say "Pastor, doing it alone doesn't work so well for me," and that person will continue to visit churches to pray. The reason of it's visitation relies on a soothing ambiance of the church and its people. Is it really soothing? Is visiting a church better than a 'secret place'?

This is absolutely not true. A person, who says that, has the eyes of the flesh and are consumed by their own mind feelings. The 'secret place' is much better than the church and it has an ambiance as well. People with desire prefer the secret place over the church. They like to be alone, rather than being a part of a crowd. They do not participate in a chatter, because, where there is an absence of words, the 'secret place of the spirit' is always ready.

"Very early in the morning, while it was still dark, Jesus got up, left the house and went off to a solitary place where he prayed" (Mark 1:35).

The Lord always prayed alone. Even during His three and a half years in the ministry, He always prayed alone despite the company of His disciples and thousands of followers. There was one exception, but other than that He always sought out the 'secret place'.

5) The second path in meeting with the Holy Spirit

Where there is a desire, a 'secret place' will be sought out. The 'secret place' is an ideal place to meet with the Holy Spirit. The place does not consider beauty or the distractions of world. There is no need to open the eyes for the beauty does not exist in this place. The mind does not need to be distracted because there are no worldly noises. You will find the place is perfect in maintaining a still heart. For this place is a refuge from the fancy world and the complication of cultures. In a same manner the 'secret place' is where humans restrain sensual desires and emotions. That is why the Lord also prayed at the secret place. Just by being still, we can sense our spirit being active in this secret place. The spirit refers to my spirit. A human being is structured by a spirit, soul and flesh. But the spirit cannot be sensed within those who live a life drenched in a worldly filth. They are flesh and soul centered. All they do and desire are chasing after the flesh and soul. When the flesh and soul are put to death, the spirit finally revives. This spirit will be able to communicate with the spirit of God. The spirit of God is the Holy Spirit. If you desire to communicate with the Holy Spirit, put to death the cravings of the flesh and the mind of the soul. What is dead does not respond. Many do not maximize the activity of the spirit, as 'busyness' and 'hurrying' begins to control the person praying in the secret place. Where there is no flesh and soul, 'busyness' and 'hurrying' also disappear. If the flesh is alive, busyness will drive one out quickly from the secret place. The thoughts are full of 'I have so much work to do, I can't stay in this secret place'. This person is at a loss in conversing with the Holy Spirit. If the soul is alive, the thoughts of hurrying will develop, soon resulting in an inability to endure the secret place. These types of people are always unstable and nerve-wracking. A buzzing fly will interfere with focusing. Or maybe a smell in the secret place will hinder your focus. These types of people cannot meet the Holy Spirit, either. Without putting death to our cravings of the flesh and thoughts of the soul, the Holy Spirit cannot be met.

The only place that our souls will become active is in the 'secret place'. Do not mistake the term 'secret place' as a designated or a specific location. The 'secret place' is available anywhere. The Lord traveled about to many different locations and ministered. And so, it cannot be only one certain location to pray in. This 'secret place' can be professed as 'a resting place for my soul'. It doesn't matter where it is. It can be the main room or a small closet. Even a bathroom is a possibility. If the focusing of your spirit can be done in that place, it is what the Lord so referred to as the 'secret place'.

A 'secret place' can be made during a walk, even in subway trains. 'Your spirit's secret place' is and always will be yours. An annoying person can prattle at you, but your rest and relaxation can be met in that 'secret place'. This can increase through practice. During your prayer of the spirit, some mosquitoes will bite you or you may hear a conflict close by. How should you react?

I call these disturbances the 'demons attacking'. Without being hindered by the outside attacks, focus more on the prayer of the spirit. Then, the spirit will find a resting secret place without even being aware of these. This is all that I am to do. A person who finds rest at the secret place of the spirit, will always be at peace, and full of hope. Without making a conscious effort to be happy, it will always result in joy.

6) The third path in meeting with the Holy Spirit

If you took endless amounts of rest at the secret place of the spirit, your spirit will still be active. Most of the desires of the flesh can be ignored easily. A mind that desires to boast, wanting to chatter, or wanting a recognition from others can immediately be stopped. You will notice this by taking a moment to re-examine yourself, to see that you have undergone a transformation. This moment is the time to meet the Holy Spirit.

If your spirit has become active, the voice of the Holy Spirit can immediately be recognized. Before, this was not so easy. But because your spirit has become active, the voice of the Holy Spirit can be identified. By hearing the voice of the Holy Spirit even once, the conversations will begin naturally. And through this, the relationship with the Holy Spirit will begin to develop. The third path in meeting with the Holy Spirit is, regardless of the task, being with the Holy Spirit. Instead of formal or traditional prayers during a meal time, try saying words of appreciation to the Holy Spirit. Some people always keep an extra empty chair. When buying a certain product, ask him which one should be bought. While doing the dishes, have a conversation with the Holy Spirit. Even ask, how much spoonful sugar should be added. Try talking to the Holy Spirit while getting in the car, or even inside the subway train. The truth is the Holy Spirit has already met with you, even if you have not met with the Holy Spirit. It is you who is not aware of this, but God and the angels have already known about it. What you should take to the heart is this truth, God is always waiting. If you do not take the initiative in searching out the Holy Spirit, the Holy Spirit will never seek you out. The problem is not that the Holy Spirit neglecting your cry. It is you who continues to argue that you did cry, when there was not a single cry.

I would like to share a dream of Pastor Kenneth E. Hagin. In his dream there were countless animals that began crowding around him. There could be seen tigers and dark apes. All these animals were in a furious rage. They rushed around Pastor Hagin, as if to kill him. When the pastor spotted Jesus on the side, he pleaded in a loud cry, "Jesus, help me … please drive them out.' But Jesus remained still and did not take a single action. As the Pastor was approaching death by being captured by the animals, he declared with a loud shout as a last resort, "In the name of Jesus Christ, be gone!" And all the animals that rushed in, began to run away. When all the animals were gone, he asked Jesus "Why did you not rescue me?" and Jesus replied, "If you do not do anything, then I don't do anything'.

Likewise, if we do not approach the Holy Spirit first, he does not draw near to us. Do not complain and say "what kind of God is this?" He himself has determined this rule. God is fine without us but we cannot live without God, right? The potter can break the pot at will, but the pot cannot command the potter.

Take the initiative on your own, and you will meet the Holy Spirit. Do not wait around. At least try extending your arm. Do something. Try the tabernacle prayer. Draw near to him. Pray the spiritual prayer, and you will find yourself meeting and conversing with the Holy Spirit.

6. Experiencing the Fire of the Holy Spirit

1) Differences in the Baptism and the Fire of the Holy Spirit

A believer of God has, at least once, been intrigued by the 'Fire of the Holy Spirit'. Even if the Fire of the Holy Spirit is new to you or you have never been interested in it, your interest will come to life through this book.

Receiving the fire of the Holy Spirit is like undergoing a miraculous phenomenon to the believers of God. The receiving of the Holy Spirit may be expressed in other words like 'Filled with the spirit'. Or can be expressed as 'anointing of the Holy Spirit'.

In the modern society, the phrase 'lets be filled with the spirit' has been so overused that this is interpreted as just living with the Holy Spirit. But, becoming filled by the Holy Spirit yields to the power of the Holy Spirit, therefore rendering authority. This is also in the scripture of Acts 1:8.

"But you will receive power when the Holy Spirit comes on you; and you will be my witnesses in Jerusalem, and in all Judea and Samaria, and to the ends of the earth." (Acts 1:8)

One thing which needs to be addressed, is that the scripture above does not refer to the baptism of the Holy Spirit but rather the anointing of the Holy Spirit. This is the Baptism of the fire. When the anointing of the Holy Spirit is received, the power from on high is also received. These things also happen during the baptism of the Holy Spirit. A greater power is received through the anointing of the Holy Spirit. When Jesus spoke these scriptures, it was not about a simple baptism of the Holy Spirit, but being filled with the Holy Spirit.

John the baptist spoke of the baptism of fire and the Holy Spirit to help clarify the differences in the scripture below.

"I baptize you with water for repentance. But after me will come one who is more powerful than I, whose sandals I am not fit to carry. He will baptize you with the Holy Spirit and with fire" (Matthew 3:11)

Why did John the baptist make a distinction from his baptism of water to Jesus' baptism of the Holy Spirit and fire?

There are various interpretations among bible scholars in reference to this scripture. But, I do understand this passage clearly. John the Baptist gave the baptism of water, but Jesus gives the baptism of the Holy Spirit and the Fire. We already know what the baptism of the Holy Spirit is. What remains is the Baptism of the Fire. This is the anointing of the Holy Spirit and points to the fire of the Holy Spirit as well.

John the Baptist possessed substantial understanding of the Holy Spirit's fire. He knew that Jesus would baptize us in the Holy Spirit and fire. As the baptism of the Holy Spirit is greater than the water baptism, the baptism of fire is greater than the baptism of the Holy Spirit.

There are degrees of differences within the baptism of the Holy Spirit and the baptism of fire. As the water baptism is different from the baptism of the Holy Spirit, the Baptism of the Holy Spirit differs from the baptism of fire. The Baptism of the Holy Spirit is important, but the baptism of the fire is of even greater importance. As the baptism of the Holy Spirit gives God's grace and brings about changes in a life with spiritual power, the baptism of fire has even greater grace, glory and power.

This baptism of fire can be expressed as a Fire of the Holy Spirit. As we can understand the water baptism, the baptism of the Holy Spirit can be understood also. As the water baptism is received through the water, so the baptism of the Holy Spirit is received through the Holy Spirit. If the water baptism belongs to the flesh, the baptism of the Holy Spirit is the spiritual. But the baptism of Fire is neither the baptism of water nor the baptism of the Holy Spirit. It is beyond these.

Within the structural framework of the tabernacle, the baptism of the Holy Spirit is done at the altar of burnt offering. The altar of burnt offering is positioned in the courtyard. The courtyard of the tabernacle is a place of preparation for worship; it isn't a place to give worship. It is because the courtyard of the tabernacle is a place of preparation for the process of becoming a true worshiper. That is why the undergoing of baptism in the Holy Spirit cannot fully mean that the receiver has become a true worshiper.

Without the water baptism and the baptism of the Holy Spirit, one cannot suddenly receive the baptism of fire. As one achieves maturity by going through the childhood phase, the baptism of Fire can only be received by first going through the water baptism and the baptism of the Holy Spirit.

If the baptism of the Holy Spirit is attained at the altar of burnt offering, then the baptism of Fire is received at the Most holy place. If the baptism of the Holy Spirit is the key essence of becoming a true worshiper, the baptism of fire, in other words the Fire of the Holy Spirit, is the key essence of a true minister. The water baptism is done with water, as the baptism of the Holy

Spirit is done through the Holy Spirit, then the Fire of the Holy Spirit is done through the anointing of oil.

The baptism of the Holy Spirit also demonstrates great power. Some speak in tongues and some offer prophesies, but some who have received the baptism of Fire demonstrate greater miracles than these. These people begin to demonstrate the healing miracles, and some begin to hear the voice of God directly.

The baptism of fire has a great power. That is why the apostle Paul confessed with full assurance that his preaching of the good news rested upon the demonstration of power by the Holy Spirit.

"because our gospel came to you not simply with words, but also with power, with the Holy Spirit and with deep conviction. You know how we lived among you for your sake" (1 Thessalonians 1:5)

Take faith. The Holy Spirit possesses tremendous authority and power. And also, believe that the baptism of the Holy Spirit comes with the fullness of the Holy Spirit.

2) Fire of the Holy Spirit and its Impartation

The Holy Spirit is often described as fire. Paul encourages with these words, "do not put out the spirit's fire" (1 Thessalonians 5:19). NIV (New International Version NIV) points out the Holy Spirit as "the fire of the spirit." In other words, the Holy Spirit is described as a fire.

"Suddenly a sound like the blowing of a violent wind came from heaven and filled the whole house where they were sitting. They saw what seemed to be tongues of fire that separated and came to rest on each of them. All of them were filled with the Holy Spirit and began to speak in other tongues as the spirit enabled them." (Acts 2:2-4).

The saints of the early church experienced the manifestation of the Holy Spirit resulting through personal witnessing. They saw the Holy Spirit splitting into a tongue of fire. John the baptist possessed the correct understanding of "fire like the Holy Spirit."

That is why he himself expressed his baptism as the "water baptism," whereas the baptism of Jesus was expressed as the "baptism of the Holy Spirit." It is more surprising that a 'baptism of fire' was mentioned with the 'baptism of the Holy Spirit."

"I baptize you with water for repentance. But after me will come one who is more powerful than I, whose sandals I am not fit to carry. He will baptize you with the Holy Spirit and with fire." (Matthew 3:11)

As we all know, John the Baptist only baptized in water. Through the water baptism, an atonement of sins was carried out, but, there were many who had not received the baptism of the Holy Spirit. That is why the Apostle Paul laid his hands on people of Ephesus for the baptism of the Holy Spirit.

And asked them, "Did you receive the Holy Spirit when you believed?" They answered, "No, we have not even heard that there is a Holy Spirit." So Paul asked, "Then what baptism did you receive?" "John's baptism," they replied" (Acts 19: 2- 3)

The Ephesus Disciples, who had received the baptism of the Holy Spirit through the Apostle Paul, began to speak in tongues and prophesied immediately. As such, the Baptism of the Holy Spirit works mightily through power. As we know, the very basis of baptism of the Holy Spirit is placed upon 'believing the Lord'. When we receive Jesus as the savior of the world and as our personal savior, we will then receive the baptism of the Holy Spirit. As we believe with our heart that Jesus is the savior, the Holy Spirit begins to manifest itself in us. When this happens, we are no longer alone, and we begin to live out our lives in walking with the Holy Spirit.

"Do you not know that your body is a temple of the Holy Spirit, who is in you, whom you have received from God? You are not your own" (1 Corinthians 6:19)

However, many Christians are not able to live out their lives in walking with the Holy Spirit. The reason is they do not recognize the Holy Spirit in them. Furthermore, it is because they have not experienced or have not worked out the powers of the Holy Spirit. A lot of people desire in walking with the Holy Spirit, in hopes of experiencing the workings of the Holy Spirit and even further, they desire to be the vessel that is filled with the power of the Holy Spirit. The baptism of fire is what enables this.

If you begin to comprehend the baptism of fire and are led to receiving this baptism, then the recognition of the Holy Spirit who dwells within us, will begin to emerge. Communication with the Holy Spirit will be enabled and you will begin to comprehend the powers of the Holy Spirit. You will undergo a vast transformation through the Holy Spirit. The words "you have changed a lot" will begin to arise from those near you. The Holy Spirit will change you as a person, while you are experiencing the power of the Holy Spirit and live in the fullness of Joy.

This is why John the baptist mentioned Jesus in giving the Baptism of the Holy Spirit and the baptism of fire. As mentioned, the baptism of fire is very important. But to our regret, many Christians are not enlightened in their understanding of the baptism of fire. How can a Christian understand the baptism of fire, when that individual has not even experienced the power of the Holy Spirit? The baptism of fire is carried out after the baptism of the Holy Spirit. Experience the mighty transformation and power through the Baptism of the Holy Spirit first. Then, experience the baptism of fire.

There were many things that did not make sense to me in the course of reading the Bible. Perhaps, you have also experienced this. Whenever this happens, I begin to ask the Holy Spirit. Then, the Holy Spirit begins to reveal the Bible, and this far surpasses the annotations or explanations regarding the Bible.

Before I had pondered on the relationship between Jesus and His Disciples. Jesus made 12 disciples and also 70 more. The works of the 12 disciples can easily be found, but the 70 others remains under a single verse mentioning.

"After this the Lord appointed seventy others and sent them two by two ahead of Him to every town and place where He was about to go" (Luke 10:1)

It is clear that Jesus sent out the 70 after having sent out the first 12 disciples. In other words, the 12 disciples were distinguished from the other 70 disciples. By observing the scene at the time of their sending, we are able to note that the disciples received 'authority' from Jesus. This authority can drive out demons, pick up snakes, and not be harmed by deadly poison, and heal sick people. Let us examine the scene where Jesus gives the authority to His disciples.

"When Jesus had called the twelve together, he gave them power and authority to drive out all demons and to cure diseases" (Luke 9:1)

Jesus gave the 12 disciples the authority and powers in driving out demons and in healing the sick. And in reality, the 12 disciples did drive out demons and heal the sick. Yes, the 70 other disciples did receive the same authority. And upon the completion of their ministry, they returned to Jesus and reported in these words.

"The seventy returned with joy and said, "Lord, even the demons submit to us in your name." (Luke 10:17)

Jesus said, "I have given you authority to trample on snakes and scorpions and to overcome all the power of the enemy; nothing will harm you" (Luke 10:19). Jesus gave the same authority to both the 12 and the 70 disciples.

Jesus had not used His godly attributes, during the course of His life on earth. It is because Jesus needed the power of the Holy Spirit in order to work out his powers (Acts 10:38). Then, what kind of power did Jesus have that allowed Him to impart such an authority to His disciples? This was the point that I could not comprehend. Then, the Holy Spirit spoke to me and told me that the authority given to the disciples by Jesus was done through an 'impartation'. This means that Jesus, having received the power and authority, shared the power and authority in Him with His disciples. Can you comprehend this?

Maybe you still think that Jesus, having used the power of His Deity, granted such an authority to His disciples. But this is not true. Not once did Jesus use His godly powers even until the death on the cross. When He was hungry, I bet that He grasped His stomach in agony. I am sure that Jesus was tempted just like the others. As such, Jesus prayed hard to receive the powers. Please refrain from thinking that Jesus had all the powers even though He did not even pray. The life of Jesus was simply a human life. Perhaps, Jesus on earth lived His life out extremely weak and poor far surpassing that of the poorest and weakest among men. It was Jesus who developed the power of the spirit of God within him by the aid of the Holy Spirit.

If the disciples of Jesus drove out the demons and healed the sick, we can also do this. Why do you think you can't do this? Are you not a disciple of Jesus? All those who profess Jesus are disciples of Jesus.

The reason behind the single mentioning of the 70 disciples in Luke 10 is because the person who needs to deliver the good news is you and I. If you look at Luke 10:2, "He told them, "The harvest is plentiful, but the workers are few. Ask the Lord of the harvest, therefore, to send out workers into his harvest field." Yes, this is true. The calling of 70 disciples by Jesus was to have them ask for people who will work. And among these 'workers of the harvest' are you and I. That is why Jesus calls everyone who believes in Him to be a disciple, thus imparting the authority mentioned below:

"And these signs will accompany those who believe in my name they will drive out demons; they will speak in new tongues; they will pick up snakes with their hands; and when they drink deadly poison, it will not hurt them at all; they will place their hands on sick people, and they will get well." (Mark 16:17-18).

Now you have come to understand that only the believers are able to receive the power and authority through Jesus. It wasn't only the 12 disciples who had received the power but the 70 disciples who are able to utilize the authority. We all can put the power and authority of the Lord to use. This is the gospel. This is the power. Hallelujah! So then, did the Lord simply speak words to impart power and authority to the disciples, or were there some other special processes involved? 'The laying on of hands is mentioned frequently throughout the Bible. In recent times, the importance of 'laying on of hands' was greatly reduced. Even some 20 to 30 years ago, everyone took great efforts in receiving a prayer through the laying on of hands. But now, if one were to carelessly lay hands on a person, that church would get in an uproar. This is how much the perception of the laying on of hands has changed.

But the power in laying on of hands in the bible is stated to be greatly powerful. Paul spoke these words to Timothy.

"For this reason I remind you to fan into flame the gift of God, which is in you through the laying of my hands" (2 Tim 1:6).

The Bible scholars do not place much importance on the laying on of hands in these verses. It is interpreted to be just an encouragement from an elder pastor to a younger pastor. However, it is most wise when the Bible is interpreted just as it is written. That is why the Ephesus Disciples receiving the Holy Spirit through the laying on of hands are mentioned in previous texts. Why would such a word as 'laying on of hands' exist, if the bible authors did not place any importance in such a word?

It is clear that Paul possessed an understanding in knowing that the power of God was imparted through the laying on of hands. In this text, Paul stated "to fan into flame the gift of God," describing the gift of the Holy Spirit as 'flame'. And the Bible scholars again interpret this text as a simple way of encouraging others to work. In the era of the early church, there were some ceremonial processes that were held as important. The author of Hebrews state such a process in the text.

"Therefore let us leave the elementary teachings about Christ and go on to maturity, notlaying again the foundation of repentance from acts that lead to death, and of faith in God, instruction about baptisms, the laying on of hands, the resurrection of the dead, and eternal judgment." (Heb 6:1 -2)

The author of Hebrews knew the things that mattered the most in living out the life of faith. That is why the author clearly states to do away with elementary teaching about Christ and to focus on things that are important. Let's look closer into the things that matter more. Aren't they truly more important?

Does the word 'laying on of hands' come into your sight? As is, the early church placed 'laying on of hands' in a high priority. This is not only important in the early church era. This is also critical within the church today and cannot be dismissed from our Christian life. In the time of the Old Testament, 'laying on of hands' was crucial. All animals brought to the tabernacle as an offering were to have hands laid on. This acted as an 'imparting of the sin'. It is only right that a sinner be burned up on the altar of burnt offerings, but God designated that an animal be burned in place of a human being, that the sins might be atoned for. During this process, the 'imparting of sins' was conducted through the laying on of hands.

In order to ordain the tabernacle priests, Moses performed a laying on of hands. This was no simple laying on of hands. The holy oil was anointed on the heads of those 'to be priests,' which were followed by 'laying on of hands'. In the world of today, we perform the laying on of hands to ordain ministers. As it can be observed, the laying on of hands is an important process that cannot be dismissed. Likewise, the laying on of hands by the father in the household of faith is carried on.

The blessings that come from the laying on of hands can only be received by those who value it. The application is similar to being redeemed by only believing in the Lord. As a person who persists in giving birth to a child by staying single is dumb, so is a person who demands payment without working. The laying on of hands can only be recognized as good, when it is performed or received through experience.

Jesus, when imparting the power and authority to the disciples, probably utilized 'laying on of hands,' and the practice was common in Israel. Through this laying on of hands, the power invested within Jesus imparted in its purity to the disciples.

The Holy Spirit commanded me to impart the anointing of the Holy Spirit through the laying on of hands. That is why I perform the laying on of hands. During this process, I undergo many different experiences. Often, I can feel a crown placed upon my head, or heat rising up toward and out of my head.

Sometimes, my head begins to tighten up or I feel a pressure in the middle of my forehead.

Besides these, my body shows many different symptoms. There are about 12 different symptoms. Each symptom varies in its meaning. And when these symptoms do appear, I am apt to find out what these symptoms mean. At first, I always asked the Holy Spirit. But as the years pass, these symptoms have become familiar to me and clear to me in nature. So, I do not ask unless it is a special case. This is by no means a rude gesture towards the Holy Spirit. If a doctor seeks out books that were previously studied in every situation, this may be a bit odd. It is extremely normal to comprehend and understand the nature of curing by experiencing its symptoms and by its effects occurring in every spiritual training process.

3) Effects of the Holy Spirit's Fire

If you have passed through the prayers of the flesh and of the mind, then being able to pray in the spirit will lead you into experiencing the fire of the Holy Spirit. As explained, the Fire of the Holy Spirit is an experience of God's glory and is also an anointing of the Holy Spirit.

Once the fire of the Holy Spirit has been received, it will yield many different gifts. Many similar gifts like prophesying or seeing are given. But, we are not sure what kind of gifts will be manifested in you. It is because these gifts are not attained by our abilities. It is only given by God to us, as we are in need of it. Eagerly desire these things, but do not petition it. Petitions are only carried out in the prayers of the flesh. There is only peace in the prayer of the spirit.

It hasn't been long since the day I started to pray in the spirit. After the worship service on a Sunday, I was meditating while sitting on the sofa. My wife laid down beside me, using my legs as a cushion, she asked me to lay my hands on her head. My eyes were still fixed on the laptop, watching a video clip from a random church. Then I proceeded to place my right hand on her forehead.

About 20 minutes had passed. My wrist on the hand that was placed on my wife's forehead began to hurt. Then the pain began to climb all the way up until my entire arm was paralyzed.

I asked the Holy Spirit about the pain and the spirit said that a powerful anointing of the Holy Spirit was poured out upon her. And these words became a reality. For a few days, my wife's entire body was completely paralyzed. After this, the hands of my wife began to burn and whenever those hands were laid upon painful areas or broken hearts, effects began to show. My wife and I began to exchange the fire on one another and spoke of our experiences.

In the course of our spiritual training session, the symptoms began to appear at a similar time frame. After 4 months had passed, as I began to lie down to sleep, my hands and feet began to burn. As this symptom was being discussed with the Holy Spirit, the spirit said that it was an outpouring of a mighty anointing of the Holy Spirit. The same symptoms began to appear on my wife on the very next day. The other symptom that began to show up was like electricity was flowing through my body. The burning and electric sensation made my hands and feet swell up. My hands and feet do not swell up anymore, but the first time I received the fire my hands swelled up so much that I could not clinch my fists. I felt so fatigued, there was not even an enough strength to open up a bottled soda. As the time progressed, my joints in my fingers felt a great amount of pain. Though the pain was alleviated over time and my strength finally returned.

As I laid my hands on other people, both hands experienced a burning sensation right away. Even when my hands were lifted up, it felt as if my hands were still upon that person and this sensation lasted awhile. Though the following sensations weren't common, when I laid my hands on a person who had been made ready, they also experienced a special type of symptoms.

A certain evangelist's left hand and wrist began to swell up as I placed my hands on the evangelist's head. It looked as if the hands were going to burst, the veins were visibly noticeable. 'Is that going to burst?' I asked the Holy Spirit, and the spirit replied, saying "it is okay, continue to place your hand on the head." Just like the words of the Holy Spirit said, the hand and the wrist began to turn normal. The evangelist asked me, "why is this happening to my left arm only?" The Holy Spirit spoke, "the right and the left hands both have a different gift." It was then, I realized that the both hands could possess different type of gifts.

To be honest, during the course of the spiritual training, I could not understand why the Holy Spirit kept saying not to clasp our hands for a prayer. Though, a habit didn't permit this, the Holy Spirit kept repeating those words. The Holy Spirit said to place our hands on the knees, with palms open and faced up. There were no particular explanations given, but this question was resolved that night. So as the spiritual training session to the disciples was carried out, the same instruction and the words of the Holy Spirit were given to them.

One day, one of the deacons under my training laid hands on a certain deacon and a minister's wife. This particular deacon had only received the training for two months. The deacon had not even heard of "Spirit" part of the Holy Spirit before, but through a book written about the Holy Spirit, that deacon attended the training session in hopes to attaining the gifts of the Spirit. To our amazement, just with 4 weeks of training, the deacon began to hear the voice of God, see visions and almighty God manifestation upon her hands laid on the deacon's head. Though the deacon was new, many began to acknowledge the powers.

And it was this day, that as a certain deacon and a minister's wife began to stagger from being drunk with the spirit, they were transmitted a surpassing amount of power when this new deacon laid her hands on them. The two spoke of the anointing in the Holy Spirit through the deacon. Many who witnessed the scene were amazed. What was really surprising was that the sensation in the right and the left hands differed from one another. One hand was in extreme pain, while the other hand felt electricity coursing through it. That day, many began to realize the truth in experiencing different sensations in the hands.

The sensation that is similar to an electric shock, a trembling feeling, or perhaps a burning sensation points to experiencing the anointing of the Holy Spirit.

The fire of the Holy Spirit can produce a trembling, electric shock, floating or body lifted, or perhaps other special sensations. But it is not necessary to distinguish these sensations, or even categorize them. If we did so, it would be placing limits on the power of the Holy Spirit.

4) Reality of the Holy Spirit

Many are wrong to misunderstand the Holy Spirit. That misunderstanding is 'fear'. Of course, whoever does not know the Holy Spirit, they would not even know what fear is. But overall, many who desire the manifestation of the Holy Spirit are afraid of meeting the Holy Spirit.

Though an eagerness may be there in wanting to talk and hear the voice of the Holy Spirit, once you do, you may well be very surprised or may even fall backwards. But meeting with the Holy Spirit occurs very naturally. An understanding may take place after an actual meeting with the Holy Spirit, but the spirit certainly doesn't work around 'fear'. It is as if seeing a very old friend, very welcoming and warm.

Another misunderstanding is thinking that the Holy Spirit is not an actual being. Even a couple of centuries ago, the belief that the Holy Spirit was a non-being was widespread. Though that thought is starting to change, some still do think that way.

The Holy Spirit is a being. As if you were talking with a friend, the Holy Spirit is that real. It is not some automated machine that pours out an electronic voice. By walking with the Holy Spirit, it has occurred to me that the spirit is a perfect being. The spirit is not strict and commanding or authoritative in treating us as lowly beings, and he does not pressure us. The spirit is always gentle, kind and warm hearted, who is ready to answer any questions that I might have. The Holy Spirit is the good teacher and guide for us all.

5) The Authority in the Fire of the Holy Spirit

Receiving the Holy Spirit's fire is like possessing the mightiest power. Do you know what makes the fire of the Holy Spirit the best power? The fire of the Holy Spirit is the power of God, which is an experience with the glory of God. If you have received the Holy Spirit's fire, you have encountered the glory of God.

When the Holy Spirit's fire is imparted to a person, a glorious occurrence takes place. Even a regular flame burns houses and is capable of burning down mountains. How much more greater the fire of God? Wouldn't it be able to burn down the entire world? The fire of the Holy Spirit has an ability to utilize the authority of God. This is the authority of God and it is what the power in the Kingdom of God is all about. God poured out the Holy Spirit and power upon Jesus, and Jesus ministered with what God poured out on him: the Holy Spirit and power.

"How God anointed Jesus of Nazareth with the Holy Spirit and power, and how He went around doing good and healing all who were under the power of the devil, because God was with Him." (Acts 10:38)

The Glory of God is all the power in that Kingdom of God. As faith represents all of God's kingdom, the glory of God is all the power in that Kingdom. By faith we enter into Heaven, but with the Glory, we experience the power of heaven. That is why the fire of the Holy Spirit becomes the very basis of foundation in faith. Without faith, no one can receive the fire of the Holy Spirit and no one can perform with power. That is why faith is all that heaven is about, becoming the very basis for power.

6) Power in the Fire of the Holy Spirit

When the fire of the Holy Spirit falls from heaven, the crippled rise to their feet. When the fire of the Holy Spirit is in working, the mountains will be tossed into the ocean. The power of the Holy Spirit's fire is incredible. Where there is the fire of the Holy Spirit, nothing is impossible. The demons cannot dwell where there is the fire of the Holy Spirit. Only the glory of God will be seen and be revealed.

Do not think that the fire of the Holy Spirit can only be manifested in a special person. Be careful of those who speak such words. The most common error in the lives of the faithful saint is that 'not everyone can receive the fire of the Holy Spirit'. Teaching that says only the select saints, special deacons and elders can receive the fire is wrong. Anyone who believes in God and confesses that Jesus is the savior can receive the fire of the Holy Spirit. If this wasn't the case, how could a person like me receive the fire of the Holy Spirit? Though, I am very careful about this topic, I am determined to speak boldly on this issue. You, too, can receive the fire of the Holy Spirit.

I recall the first days of receiving the fire of the Holy Spirit. There was a tremendous delight in healing even the smallest ills. One day, my wife asked me to place hands on her ankle. I was not aware that the fire of the Holy Spirit was already manifested in me. But when she did request to be laid hands on, I did it with faith and listened to the voice of the Holy Spirit.

It was not even a month since the first day I heard the voice of the Holy Spirit. A conversation with the Holy Spirit had already begun in those times, but having the power to cleanse sicknesses and diseases had not even occurred to me.

The ankle of my wife had shattered into pieces around the celebration time of the elder son's baby shower. There were surgeries and therapies but after those operations, she was not able to stand on her feet for long. We could not even imagine having her jump or run around with her injury. Eventually, she began to gain weight, and with the weight came more pain on her ankles. That day was the same, her ankle was in a great pain, which urged her to ask for the laying on of hands. With the love for my wife, my hands were laid on her ankle. I had never done this before. I had mixed feelings. I felt troubled and foreign to this concept. Furthermore, I began to worry. "What if it doesn't heal?" But by taking courage, my focus was on hearing the voice of the Holy Spirit.

Suddenly, the Holy Spirit spoke these words: "declare." Being caught by surprise, I responded with "yes, what?" And the Holy Spirit gave the following phrase:

"In the name of Jesus of Nazareth, ankle, be healed to its normal state!"

As if I was reading them, the words were declared slowly and with precision. Then, the Holy Spirit spoke once again: "declare once again." The phrase was declared two more times, totaling three in all. After the third declaration, the Holy Spirit told me to remove my hands. In obedience, I did lift my hands from my wife's ankle.

She began to walk around and said that she was not hurting anymore. She even began to run around. Prior to this, even with a slight movement, she began to suffer from the pain in her ankle but now she was even dancing. By turning on some music, she began to dance with the elder son who was standing next to us. God had healed her ankle. Hallelujah!

Ever since that day, her ankle has not felt a problem. There were times in the start of our church service, where she stood at the register for long hours. At times she did confirm that her ankles were little agitated, but this was a very light pain, and every time she spoke of her ankles troubling her, I held the ankles and imparted the fire of the Holy Spirit, which immediately dissipated the pain. Her ankles were healed enough that we moved all our furniture with a crew of three, my father-in-law, my wife, and myself.

7) Character of God

As mentioned earlier, the fire of the Holy Spirit is the Glory of God. Yes, where there is a God, and the glory of God dwells within that place. There is glory because there is God. We are the children of God. The children are bound to be influenced by their fathers. As such, when the father has a glory, the children also possess a glory. If the father was a president, then the children would be the children of a president.

Who is your father? Is it not God? If you so believe that God is your father, you are already a child of God and thereby possessing the glory of God. The same can be spoken of in terms of possessing the authority of God: you already have it, because the authority of God is meant to be implemented by both God and the child of God.

"Yet to all who received Him, to those who believed in His name, He gave the right to become children of God" (John 1:1 2)

"Now if we are children, then we are heirs--heirs of God and co-heirs with Christ, if indeed we share in his sufferings in order that we may also share in His glory." (Romans 8:17)

If you are a child of God, then both the character and authority of God will be manifested in you. First, understand the character of God and apply those characteristics completely to yourself. That is when the authority of God will begin to show. The authority of God rises when the fire of the Holy Spirit is received, but without the character of God, there can be no fire of the Holy Spirit.

It only makes sense to know that the character of God shows in a person who has received the fire of the Holy Spirit. If a person continues to love the things of this world even after claiming to have received the fire of the Holy Spirit, that fire is not of the Holy Spirit. If that person, having received the fire, continues to love the desires of flesh, lust of the eyes and boasting of this world, then the fire is of the devil. Remember! A person without a hint of godly character in their lives possesses a false fire. Do not look into fires of that person. First, look and see if that person possesses a godly character.

The fire of the Holy Spirit is very precious to the church. As the church is the body of Christ, a true church must show the character and authority of Christ. If a church is consistently cheating and is full of thieves, that church is no longer a church. Rather, that church can be seen as an institution for breeding thieves and cheaters. If members of the church are adulterers and craving lust, that church is not a member of Christ's body, but rather a hoax club. The fire of the Holy Spirit burns such things of this world, and it will burn off all that is not pure for the church. There will be the glory of God through the fire of the Holy Spirit. The name of Jesus will be lifted high through the fire of The Holy Spirit.

As Christ made the church as his body, church is to possess a pleasing aroma of Christ by being the arms and leaving the footprints of Christ. That aroma is the very product of being filled with the Holy Spirit, the fire of the Holy Spirit. The Fire of the Holy Spirit makes the body of Christ known in this world and for the people to breathe in the very aroma of Christ.

7. Listening to the voice of God

1) The utmost in experiencing the Glory

Moses talked with God at the atonement cover.

"When Moses entered the tent of meeting to speak with the LORD, he heard the voice speaking to him from between the two cherubim above the atonement cover on the ark of the testimony. And he spoke with Him" (Numbers 7:89).

"There, above the cover between the two cherubim that are over the ark of the Testimony, I will meet with you and give you all my commands for the Israelites" (Exodus 25:22).

Moses heard the voice of God at the atonement cover. The atonement cover is where the glory of God dwelled. The pillar of cloud covered the tent of meeting and the pillar of fire shone upon the ark of the covenant. As the atonement cover acts as the lid of the ark of the covenant, the blood of Jesus was sprinkled upon the cover.

This atonement cover was so holy that even the high priest, Aaron, was not permitted entry.

"The LORD said to Moses: "Tell your brother Aaron not to come whenever he chooses into the Most Holy Place behind the curtain in front of the atonement cover on the ark, or else he will die, because I appear in the cloud over the atonement cover" (Leviticus 16:2)

Moses heard the voice of God at the atonement cover. Was it only Moses who was able to hear the voice of God? We are the children of God, just as Moses is a child of God. Wouldn't it be possible for us to hear the voice of God, if Moses heard so?

It is clear that Moses heard the voice of God at the atonement cover. But, the atonement cover does not exist in this world anymore. There is no ark of the covenant in this world anymore. There is no tabernacle of Moses anymore. The temple is placed within our body.

The temple in our body also has the altar of burnt offerings and the wash basin. There is the holy place and the most holy place as well. At the altar of burnt offerings, the baptism of the Holy Spirit will take place and cleanse our conscience. At the wash basin, the baptism of water will be carried out in cleansing our bodies. The Holy place will be a place of worship in purifying the spirit, and the Most Holy place will be a place of experiencing the glory of God.

We must enter into the spiritual ark of the covenant daily. We have to experience the glory of God in that place. In that place, we will have to receive the fire of the Holy Spirit and progress in experiencing the ever-greater glory of God.

Listen to the voice of God. As Moses has done, so incline your ears. Are you aware that Joshua heard the voice of God? How about Abraham, who heard the voice of God? How about David, who heard the voice of God? Elijah and Elisha, do you know that they also heard the voice of God? Are you aware that Isaiah and Ezekiel heard the voice of God? How about the Apostle Peter and Paul, do you know that they heard the voice of God? Do you know that even a normal believer like Ananias and a gentile like Cornelius heard the voice of God?

There is no verse that forbids us from hearing the voice of God. It is nowhere to be found. Rather, the scriptures say that without hearing the voice of God, maintaining a righteous life is impossible. Listen to the voice of God. Desire it eagerly. If God is your father, why can a child not hear the voice of God?

I am reminded of Jesus' Words.

"The watchman opens the gate for him, and the sheep listen to his voice. He calls his own sheep by name and leads them out" (John 10:3).

A child is bound to hear the voice of the father. It is only odd that one is not able to hear the voice of God, Listening to the voice is not mystical. Of course, the voice may differ from a person to person. Some may understand simply through their feelings, just like knowing your loved one's feelings without exchanging words. To some, it may come through a sign, which is like a burning sensation, or a peaceful mind when doing the right thing. Or maybe like experiencing dizziness, pain or anxiousness, when doing the wrong thing. Then, there are some who hear the voice. This voice cannot be described as a person carrying on a conversation with someone. It is because the voice can only be heard between you and God. When Jesus received a baptism from John the Baptist, a voice came from heaven.

"and the Holy Spirit descended on him in bodily form like a dove. And a voice came from heaven:

"You are my Son, whom I love; with you I am well pleased." (Luke 3:22)

What is striking is that the voice of God was only heard by Jesus, the others couldn't hear it. Not even John the baptist could hear this voice of God. His affirmation did not come from the voice from heaven, but by witnessing the Holy Spirit descending like a dove.

"Then John gave this testimony: "I saw the spirit come down from heaven as a dove and remain on him. I would not have known him, except that the one who sent me to baptize with water told me, 'The man on whom you see the spirit come down and remain is he who will baptize with the Holy Spirit.' (John 1:32-33)

There are people who cannot hear the voice of God, even by standing next to a person who hears the voice of God. It is simply because a true worship is made between God and that specific person through a personal relationship. That is why the most holy place could only be entered by the high priest. Only one person can enter into the most holy place, and even now only one person is permitted to enter.

Experiencing the most holy place means experiencing the presence and the Glory of God. Just like feeling of the clouds filling in the entire space of the most holy place, and the glory of God being felt. Even if the clouds show the glory of God by filling up the Most Holy Place, it is no comparison to the actual glory of God shining upon the ark of the covenant. Enter into the ark of the covenant. Enter into it everyday. If you do enter into the Ark of the Covenant, the Cherubs protecting the very first part of the ark of the covenant will know. As you experience the glory of God through the blood at the Atonement cover, in no time will you begin to sense becoming one with God.

Chapter 3

....

Testimony of the Tabernacle Prayer

Grandmother, mom and a son's tabernacle prayer.

It was a Friday, I was heading to see mom at my side of the family. The voice of God was clear while in the car with Jung Min. It felt as if hearing the voice inside the head was being well grasped. Having laid down on the bed after the tabernacle prayer resulted in a clearer voice of God. Now, having prayed twice with a leader gave an assurance in acknowledging the voice of God. The determination in sharing this grace with my mother swelled up and not desiring to lose this frequency, I quickly headed there.

"Mom!" the door of the house flung open. Mom's facial expression felt welcoming. Mom had always longed for the most holy place of God. She has been a widow, who had thirsted after the voice of God. It had been about a week of sharing this grace, but after the last night's sharing, the desire for the tabernacle prayer became the main focus.

About 9 o'clock evening time, Mom, Jung Min, and I sat together. The three generations. We as three members had searched everywhere, desiring this grace. God had gathered the three generations once again now for this tabernacle prayer. Thanks to God for this grace! A brief explanation to Mom was given, who is familiar with the structure of the Tabernacle. And to Jung Min, pictures were drawn so that the procedure could be explained in detail.

In such a short time I had become a leader. I was the only person who was familiar with the tabernacle prayer process ... ... Through the sprinkling of the blood at the gate of the Tabernacle and Jung Min crying in tears at the altar of burnt offering ... As if tears were shed for a loss of a loved one, I cried out. Jung Min spoke of experiencing a certain feeling of himself praying upon the altar of burnt offering. "Mom, there is a stinky smell, an odd stench ... sniff sniff ... it stinks, so terrible, it's horrible." He was crying again due to the smell. "It will disappear at the wash basin, feel the fire." I continued to lead the process.

All of a sudden, as if a tear gas had been released, my throat began to feel cottoned up in coughs instead of my own desire in speaking words. Satan's interference was too severe. The blood was sprinkled in between the process to and from the wash basin. The stench and the burning sensation of tear gas began to disappear. And because it was Jung Min's first time, the flow of the process kept getting interfered by his questions.

By re-gathering the focus, we headed to the wash basin. Jung Min's endless repenting of sins were suddenly turned into a dry puking, he was continuously crying. I had told him to spit it out, but he kept on swallowing instead. Without a moment to spare, I sat him in front and with my hands upon his chest and stomach, I began to repent. And in some time passing, things began to puke out after a severe dry puke. It was done through me instead of Jung Min. I calmed him down and asked for his continuous focus.

With Jung Min's continuous questions and events, I felt sorry in witnessing my inability to focus on my mother's face. Jung Min begins to speak of a vision, in seeing Jesus washing him down at the wash basin. It was amazing to see Jung Min, who was continuously breaking up the spiritual flow, seeing visions so well. But was it real?

I saw the jar of water being lifted up to be poured out. At the bread of presence prayer, we gave a fervent intersession prayer and Jung Min could see himself eating the bread. And the Holy Spirit was invited at the Golden Lamp stand.

The Golden Jar of Manna – Jung Min spoke of people dying and the jar breaking into pieces suddenly. (I could not comprehend this, so we kept asking the Holy Spirit. An understanding came about in a death of an ego and idols breaking up in pieces. And only by then, would faith become like a purified gold. And the jar would be able to store up the words of truth like the water jars used at the wedding ceremony at Cana).

Stone Tablets – Jung Min spoke of 'Ten commandments'. While hearing the word, 'Love'. Staff – Jung Min spoke of 'Faith'. I heard 'Life'. Mom said that she wasn't sure.

Mom was standing in the cloud, light and fire, and she said that the moment reminded her of the words that were spoken to her at her time of first belief. That the first moment of believing involved visions of heaven opening up with a ray of light shining down, and within the light a tall and smaller man weeping in tears. And the voice that followed after was "Love the Lord your God with all your heart, soul and might." After having witnessed this scene, my mother began to follow Jesus. And she spoke of the current moment as undergoing the same experience like the first believing moment in her life.

Jung Min, with a continuous stream of questions that broke up the flow of spirit and focus, rather appeared to receive all the grace that was being poured out. As for myself, uncontrollable dryness in the throat and coughs kept attacking me, which made me cling unto the blood of Jesus.

This was a time of Manifestation. Jung Min looked as if struck by the mighty presence of God, who began to lay down on the floor. He spoke of seeing clouds and the ray of light shining down upon his chest. Then, he spoke of the light turning into a fire, which manifested in his mind. "Mom! My left arm is in extreme pain. I can't move it as if paralyzed. I am Scared!." "Do not be afraid, he is healing and giving you powers. I will ask the pastor for you." Having calmed him down initially, he spoke of his right arm being pressed down, in weakness and shaking. Even his legs felt weighed down as if a boulder sat upon it.

Then, he spoke with his eyes open. "Mom, I see the clouds and planes flying. Inside the plane I see Jesus and myself! We are flying and this scene looks like a photograph!" I decided to ask the pastor after the prayer session, in regards to Jung Min seeing visions correctly and how he could see those things in his first tabernacle prayer.

Jung Min spoke of a voice that kept coming into his mind, "your arm will heal, you will be filled with happiness." Then he said "I am unsure, perhaps those words are just my thoughts. But, I keep hearing these words!" After this phase, he spoke of hearing "Demons cannot enter into you. Keep sprinkling the blood of Jesus everyday. Your arm will heal." Then, he said he experienced a difficulty in breathing and being stuffed up in his chest.

These circumstances brought about a great confusion to mom and I. We had spent our mind on the effects occurring in Jung Min. "I see lights that are yellow and Red. When I said 'Glory of God', I see the blue light shining out from my mind. The light is growing, my left arm that felt paralyzed and cramped ... right now, it feels a lot lighter. Only my wrist feels focused with a burning sensation."

As soon as the tabernacle prayer ended, the dry throat and coughs began to disappear. There came about a greater understanding in interceding for the leaders undergoing attacks during the course of the tabernacle prayer.

I wrote out an instruction with a drawing for mom to pray the tabernacle prayer, so that it could be done by herself. No greater depth could be reached today by praying with Jung Min, but mom spoke of her determination in wanting to do the prayer by herself. With such a desire, I know she will succeed.

The tabernacle prayer with the three generations coming into an end, I was still curious. Did Jung Min really hear the voice of God? What are the effects that came about on his left arm? Did he really see visions with his eyes open? Today, it was as if Jung Min had met his day of fortune.

Special tabernacle prayer experience

My mind is only joyful as the time of tabernacle prayer draws near. Praises of God continues to echo through my inner being. To be truthful, I am praying because of a financial problem, not of joyful situations. But, my mind continues to praise with "thank you, I am full of joy." And because this situation weighs down heavily, normally, these things would only result in endless sighs and in an inability to study. 'Was it because of the pastor's wife's impartation? And am I not being too joyful?'

Finally, it is a time to pray the tabernacle prayer. With a great anticipation, I logged on early and got connected. Jumping ahead, I read through the praise lyrics, being convinced that the praise was chosen for me. By sprinkling the blood of Jesus, I entered through the gate of the tabernacle. The altar of burnt offering was built with a stone and as if it had burnt up many things, the altar was covered with many burnt marks. I was kneeled down upon the altar of burnt offering, a thought glimpsed in wanting to burn up all that is within me. I was pulling out pouches from my body. "Lord, here is pride, Lord here is greed." And like this, I was pulling out the pouches in front of me. And as if I was shedding out my skin, I took my body and laid them beside the pouches. I was waiting for the Fire of the Lord. And to my amazement, only the things that I had laid down were burned up by the fire that came down from above. "Lord. Burn me up as well." And a reply could be sensed, "The things to be burned up were all given and laid down, weren't they?"

By moving unto the wash basin, my face was covered with a smile. I am to be in a despair of the things that need to be repented for, but rather a smile was coming from looking unto the Father, who would forgive my sins. I was thankful, rather than being in despair of my sins during its repentance. I repented, and asked for his forgiveness, and with a continual "thank you," my face resonated with a smile.

With the tabernacle prayer leader, we moved unto the bread of presence. There was a round bread that had been puffed up. It was reaching up to the ceiling. I asked the Holy Spirit why this scene was being witnessed, but there was no reply.

Then, at the golden lamp stand, we invited the Holy Spirit and began to pray in tongues. I was confessing in my heart, "Lord, I love you, I want to love you more. I want to be filled with the love that surpasses all things in this world. A love so pure that is not comparable to a love between a man and a woman. A love so great that cannot be compared to a love of family members. A love that could not be experienced in world. That love is what I want to have with you Lord."

Soon, the voice of the tabernacle prayer leader could not be heard. But without wavering, I approached the atonement cover and as my leader would always do, I envisioned sprinkled of the Lord's blood on my body in meditation of the cross.

Then, I entered the Ark of the Covenant. Inside the ark, there could be seen the three relics. I could see myself eating the manna by opening the golden jar of manna. My physical body could not sense any taste, but I could witness myself eating with a great appetite. And I was witnessing myself looking through the relics, then by jumping up, I began to play by pushing the Ark of the Covenant around. It felt uneasy on me and I began to grow suspicious of the vision, as if it was a correct vision. Then, I was hugging the ark of covenant and soon laying on it. Then, I was already on my knees beside the ark of covenant. I was watching myself with a joyful and happy smile on my face, and a cloud began to envelope around me. It looked liked a peaceful prayer in the cloud. Then I witnessed myself being hugged by the Lord, wouldn't this to be the fulfillment of my hope?

I began to dance about in praises to the Lord, in wanting to make the Lord happy. "My soul sings with joy, my soul praises joyfully." A praise that could not be thought of were being sung and danced around, I was simply watching myself doing these things. "hahahahaha" I could feel God's laughter, rather than hearing it.

I could see myself thinking that the praising and dancing should soon come to a stop, in choosing to pray through holiness.

And there was me, kneeling down to the Lord, in wanting to lift up prayers. But that prayer seemed as if I was trying to think of painful and sorrowful things, so that I could speak with the Lord.

Then, the Lord's reply was heard. It cannot be recalled in exact words but he said something like this, "it is okay, do not try to speak up forcefully. Isn't today the first day of having you inside the Holy place? Isn't it special that you are full of thankfulness? Let us be more joyful! And be merry!." He seemed very happy as if it was a great event of a remembrance.

Tabernacle prayer with Eun Bin

Becoming a registered as a member of the internet café site, why was my heart so excited ... Perhaps it was my weaknesses that caused the trembling to riptide. But an understanding was given, that the feeling wasn't from the Lord.

Even my husband, who is a pastor, had promised to join me today but was delaying it a bit. Which caused a bit of an emotional downfall. But there is an understanding that wanted me to wait patiently in being comforted; and not get involved through those emotions. Pastor David Lee's praise music on "blood of Christ" were echoing as I waited patiently. Then, Eun Bin (Senior in high school) opened the door of the room with a smile and said "Mom! I am home" and began to sing along "Lord's blood has power. Lord's blood covers me." "Eun Bin, would you like to pray the tabernacle prayer with me? If you are too tired, you could sleep." Eun Bin replied,

"okay, let me get cleaned up real quick." Then he exited the room.

A couple of days ago, I was sharing the experiences occurring during the tabernacle prayer with the pastor. All of a sudden, Eun Bin came beside me, saying "Mom. Really? How about me? How about my soul? Did he take my soul along as well? Why didn't you take me?" and proceeded to hug me. "Of course, you were taken along as well Eun Bin." "What did the Lord say?." "Lord says he loves you so much and waits for you, he seems a bit sad because you don't love him as much lately ... What do you think about this Eun Bin?." "I know this as well, ok, I do feel it too." "Let's start praying the tabernacle prayer. Eun Bin, you did agree. Mom is waiting too, when will your heart be ready for this?"

I came back into the room with a small smile on my face and it seems to have stirred the heart. The tabernacle prayer began. I could not focus, because all of my attention was gathered on Eun Bin. In Spirit, I was holding the hands of Eun Bin. Eun Bin was following the prayer leader, but the shuffling of a posture and vivid movements could be seen. By sprinkling the blood of Jesus, prayer for attention and focus were being declared. When our personal petitions ended, we replied to the sound of the leader's prayer with an Amen.

Amen was loud and clear in inviting the Holy Spirit at the golden lamp stand. Prayer of tongues were done loudly at the altar of incense. As time passed on, the prayer of tongue became a bit quieter and occasionally came to a halt. But, I was still thankful. The blood of the Lord was sprinkled, as the leader spoke words of prophesy and began to sing in tongues. The leader said that the Gift of praise in tongue was given to Eun Bin and kept on prophesying. Without losing a moment, Eun Bin continued to reply with the words of Amen in tears. I could not cease or stop from shedding tears. I asked Eun Bin as the tabernacle prayer session ended.

"How was it?"

"I am not completely sure yet. To be honest, I fell asleep from time to time."

"I knew that. But you were lead to the end of life. I figured you would sleep during the middle. Why did you cry there?"

"Umm, well~ Jesus said that he loves me, and I felt so thankful ... I couldn't even focus during the prayer time and there isn't even one good thing in his sight that I have done. But he says he planned, protected and leads me and that he loves me. Mom! At the wash basin, there was a well, a deep well, I repented and swam in there!"

Eun bin expressed the desire in talking with the prayer leader and asked a couple of questions. Those Questions were answered and appeared to have satisfied his need. "Lord~ Thank you!."

Sweet time of fellowship with the Holy Spirit

Yesterday was the first session of tabernacle prayer led by Lovefountain leader. It had only been a few days since the introduction to the tabernacle prayer website. I was never fond of the internet, so everything felt very rigid. However, it was the enduring love and grace of God and the Holy Spirit in Jesus towards me that enabled reading of the writings in becoming a participant of the 4th tabernacle prayer call out.

I am a pastor's wife residing at the state of Georgia in America. My husband had ministered as an assistant pastor in New York but came down here, after having heard the voice saying, "You have taught church members that led to evangelization but have you personally evangelized to a single soul for the saving of their souls?"

As often spoken, "Lack of awareness often leads to boldness," none of us had possessed any prior knowledge in starting a church without having a single member having committed; we simply came down with a sole passion for the love in God. Soon, we began to experience an abundant blessing of God through strength and bravery that worked in us during the founding phase of ministry, hence witnessing the fruits of evangelism. But as of right now, we are taking a little break from the three years spent in ministry. By reading Lee Jung Ae's spiritual journal (Rev. David Lee's wife), we came to an agreement in their ministry experiences at the Denver location. We are reviewing the causes that resulted in taking a break from ministering and are waiting for God to provide an answer to our prayers.

I wasn't born into a Christian family, but had met Jesus three years prior to marriage. I simply desired God and liked Him. And during the process of striving in how one could know God more, I met my husband. The marriage decision was solely on seeing a life that lived out in faith, which I was thankful of. And by moving down to his seminary school in America, the life as a pastor's wife, as a Christian, had begun at the school campus dormitory.

Pastor's wives who prayed a lot in resulting spiritual gifts often resulted to me in a downcast.

But as a response, I held unto God who seeks out hearts; enduring with a pure, unchanging love and passion. Gift in speaking of Tongues were received about 7 to 8 years ago, but whenever others spoke of dreams and visions, I often pondered in a greater desire with "Why wouldn't God allow these things to me?" And the things that seemed to be fogged up, began to clear up through the 'Walk with Bible' group. It wasn't long ago that I had felt my hands turning hot during the deeper prayer sessions. My body usually keeps colder temperatures but the effects would turn up when engaged in a prayer. And the sensations in my hands moving about in the ark of covenant prayer began to be noticed. So, one day, I just decided to let my arms go, which resulted in my arms moving about very slowly up and down. Because, there was no prior knowledge regarding these effects, I just figured it was pretty cool and forgot about it.

After registering to a tabernacle prayer session, I began to pray with the mp3 prayer sessions on the website during the prayer session wait time. On the first day of the session, while praying in front of the Ark of the Covenant, my lips began to tremble. Before the session, I had read Rev. David Lee's writings and because of this foreknowledge, I just let my body wait patiently, even though my lips were a bit paralyzed.

"Holy Spirit, I know that I am impatient but even though the session is being followed, I do not see clouds, lights or can't even sense the fire. I am merely drawing mentally as I hear and why can't I hear your voice?"

It wasn't a voice but a message came about in my heart, "You have been filling your ears with the things of this world, and that is why you can't hear me." A quick repentance was made, followed by a determination. After this, two of the mp3 prayer sessions were lifted up but nothing happened. Yesterday, the very first session of 4th call out Tabernacle prayer began. A great effort was exerted in keeping the eyes on the Lord that desires pureness and not doing the things that the Holy Spirit hates, such as being impatient.

Without any noticeable encounters, the tabernacle prayer session ended in grace. With a bit of feeling at loss, I forced myself to stand up (Prayer session was already over and had concluded with the words of Amen). As my heart yearned for wanting to pray in tongues, I sat back down and began to pray in tongues through repentance of the sins that I had committed, which were long forgotten. Then, a sudden sensation over took my body.

My hands were already hot, but my arms began to twitch a little. Like the first day of prayer session, my lips began to move about resulting in bringing about a great smile on my face. I began to engage in a conversation with the Holy Spirit as my heart was caught up in a laughter. No voices were heard but a sense in my soul communicating with the Holy Spirit in deep depth could be noticed.

Great laughter in a one moment but in another moment an angry persons' expression of mouth came about over and over again, then my neck began to turn with my arms rotating. A great duration of time was spent in kneeling down, so I spoke "Holy Spirit, my legs hurt a lot." Then, my posture was fixed from kneeling down to lying on my back. All these movements came about very slowly.

In a fear of not waking up in time the next day, I said "Holy Spirit, I must sleep now." With a complaint and with a hint of love, I began to arrange the place of prayer. Two hours had passed already. Even as I lay on the bed, my hands were burning and my body began to twitch. Even though the Holy Spirit had been residing in me, it felt as if the Holy Spirit was moving about the house reorganizing and rearranging as the new owner moves into a house to see if all the doors were functioning properly, in a great happiness and joy.

The happiness was overwhelming, I spoke to the Holy Spirit "I am all yours Holy Spirit, all my body is yours, please rest from moving about and help me fall asleep." With a joyful complaint, I fell asleep. Even though I was asleep, a sense of knowing that the Holy Spirit continuing to move through the places resided. For a while, no deep sleep could be brought about but was awake from the sleep due to bodily jerks happening from time to time.

As I write, my confusions regarding the works of the Holy Spirit are beginning to make sense. Today, on the way back home driving, I cried out loudly in remembrance of the calling that was given me. The heart of God that cries out in a painful rending toward the world that is coming to a destruction was made known to me, I cried out as a response, "God, send me, Use me." I am strengthen again, there are no more fears and there remains no confusion. "Lord, hold me tight. I am coming to you. Hallelujah!"

Discipleship training

Due to the Christmas event preparation, worship dance and praise practices filled my Fridays. Even the 18th day of the month felt a little out of control due to practices. From 2pm to 4pm involved praise practices and the tabernacle prayer was carried out from 4pm to 5pm. All the young participants enjoyed the tabernacle prayer. Everyone was amazed at the speed of time having gone by. They were filled with joy. Through the repeated prayer sessions, the young group began to shape-up. If they were told that it was a prayer training session, even under the stressful situations the young ones began to move in an organized and orderly manner. Of course, it was always conducted through the leader of a group.

It felt as if I was the only one passionate during the Saturday prayer session. The passionate heart of the Lord toward these children and his tears were felt so strongly that I was praying with unceasing tears falling from my eyes accompanied by a runny nose. When this type of focus kicks in, it is hard to oversee the young group's prayer behavior in correcting and educating them. Regardless, the prayer session made me feel good.

1st grade student's prayers are always fervent. Some of them looked a bit exhausted from the continuous worship and from the training. Though, some asked for more prayer time after having played around. I mentioned that anyone who prays under compulsion, not because they want to but have to, could go home. After giving them a little while; the group members started to leave with many different excuses. To my surprise, the members who had stayed were all involved in the discipleship training (this training group was intended upon having 12 members, including the 5 initial members). But even those who were qualified did not want to join a group that required memorizing the Ten Commandments with 5 verses and do an early Morning Prayer for 5 consecutive days with many other things. That was the reason why the rest remained distant, in all honesty, this group's training sessions did not see much success in gathering together. Though, recently an improvement in meeting together could be noticed. The 1st grade disciple group had a kid named Sung Sup, who was asking in a great intent for my authorization in being excused to go home.

"Sure, you can go."

"Wow, really?"

"Yes, but where would you go?"

"Where my mom is, (Praise group wait room), but I do want to attend the prayer training session."

"That is not possible."

"Why so?"

"Well, the training session lasts until 6pm. With the prayer training lasting until 5pm, you can't just stop praying in the middle and go home. If you want to leave, you can go now or get the full training until 6pm! Okay?"

(With a brief moment of silence) "Well, I must pray the repentance prayer, so I will stay." How cute and lovely! The kids are so good at reciting the tabernacle prayer phrases during the prayer session. And, even the replies of Amen are well done. Now, it is me who needs to get up to a good level. As a person who shouldn't be standing as a leader, it is my serious concern in seeing about how I stand before them.

Tabernacle (the ark of covenant) Prayer with the Lord

The altar of burnt offerings began to emit a very dark smoke. The Lord was speaking to me about the color of sins.

The Lord washed out my hair with a pure water from the wash basin. Even the leader was saying that the Lord was washing each one of us. The way in which the Lord moved about his hands were full of grace and friendliness. Also the way in which these hands washed our feet moved in a similar manner.

The leader told us to focus at the bread of presence. By looking up to it, there was the Bible laid on top of the table. His words of life ... with these words, Matthews 7:7 was given. God wanted us to ask about the things of this world, the problems of life and the good things, including the Holy Spirit, to be sought out within the scriptures. The Bible was an answer to the mankind, who seeks and desires all things. The answers of all my questions are surely laid out within these scriptures!

By the authority given me, I began a powerful prayer against the enemies, which was accompanied by the Blood of the Lord prayer. Spiritual forces of evil and powers of the dark world, the spirits that work in those who are disobedient were all tied up in being casted, in which their strongholds began crumbling down. The spirits that work within generations, spirits of curse, bitter roots of spirituality, all types of spirits were sprinkled and covered by the blood. The Lord was wanting to cover all the aspects life through the sprinkling of Blood, entirely relying on him.

"Lord, help in pulling out the bitter roots within me. Burn it with the fire of the Holy Spirit. Wash out with water, which are your words, to be pure through the Lord's precious blood."

The prayer of tongue went about a continuous change at the altar of burnt offerings, as it was encouraged to pray with a power and speed. The very first voice of the Lord was heard, "I am delighted" as the leader spoke the following words.

"The Lord just said, 'My Dear Son, I am delighted.'"

I was mistaken in perceiving that the most holy place was caught on fire. The very corners of the tent were caught on fire as the clouds of glory settled upon the place. As the blood of Lord from the Cross began to fill up the place, I could see the movement like a small rippling of water starting to rise up. Rising higher still, slowly. By being completely submerged, I could witness myself wearing a white linen robe. The leader spoke up.

"Our clothes have been changed into a white linen robe."

I could see the Lord smiling upon me from inside the Ark of the Covenant. The leader spoke up simultaneously, the Lord is smiling upon us. Like this, many same experiences were encountered with the Leader. Of course, there are different experiences too, perhaps from differing interpretations and perceptions. Above all, as the Leader leads, its followers begin to see the drawings and soon it begins to pull through. And these things begin to be accepted with confidence and assurance. As if, a son begins to understand the fathers voice …At the ark of covenant, my hands pulled out a scroll from the Ten Commandments. The scroll contained Leviticus 19:2.

"Be Holy because I am Holy."

About 2 years ago, at the Shin University (Korean University) dormitory, I had experienced my spirit separating from the body during sleep. I saw myself in the spirit. At that moment I was sitting on a floating chair beside the bed in midair. And, there was another being sitting behind me! I was terror struck. The initial thought was that it could be either a demon or Jesus. Coincidentally, the chair was made out of a plastic and the arm-rest was bent like a sickle pressuring down on my stomach. It was very painful and un-comforting.

So, I asked the being to stretch out the bent arm-rest. My reasoning was that if it was Jesus, that being could stretch out the bent piece. To my expectation, the being stretched out the piece through his big hands. I could see the being's hands, and he spoke.

"As the Sabbath is holy, I desire your life to be holy."

Hallelujah! Within a 7 year span, I experienced the separation of the spirit 5 times occurring through a trance. But every time this happened, words were given. Should it be compared to a clear rushing sound of water? Or to a sound of an Angel? But the times of rebuking, sounded like a mighty noise from a cave. The feelings of reverence and fear accompanied the voice, as if it was only me and Him in this world. Out of the words given, the voice that spoke beside my ear still rings vividly.

"Do you love me more than the others?"

As I re-entered the most holy place, the leader exited. And a giant like back of Jesus took me up and began to fly around the sky. By flying through the plains and mountains, I could see a gathering of mighty multitude within a far distance on a wide plain, like a conference location. Out of the multitude, in the front area stood a person with a great green flag. I realized that the person in front was me. It was zoomed in to my eyes from a great distance.

As I focused again, I was in the space and Jesus said to look unto the Earth. As it was black like the color of the space, it could only be differentiated by looking at it closely. The Lord said that it was the spirit of darkness and the Earth was covered by it. Like a firefly, there were lights resonating within the parts of the earth but the darkness, the very dark of it covered the entire world. The Lord said that it was the last hour.

And the Lord began to show the after effects of the restoration, like a drawing, it began to change to a great blue and white color. It was a magnificent scene of the nature. Hallelujah! How much do you desire me? I am all that you are. How much do you hunger after me? I am the bread of life. How much do you thirst after me? I am the water that wells up within you, the source of living water.

I will begin to manifest my love in abundance to your life through the revealing of my name. The hunger, thirst and desire will never be quenched in you. Through the pure living water welling up, you will have my heart and through it, you will love.

The true love of the Spirit will begin to be taught in you and you will learn to share it. Your eyes will open up in seeking the verse, "As I have loved you."

The things I have taught you, prophesy worship, praise and the intercessory prophesy will become the core part of Church. My hidden manna will be tasted and like the eyes of an eagle in being able to gain a spiritual insight and revelation in seeing the hour of a generation will be given to you. On one hand, the restoration of truth, on the other, power of God will be given in yielding these powerful weapons of righteousness through the heavenly strategies upon you.

Focus, pay attention. Keep on walking. I am your God. Do not confess in flesh or soul but confess in the Spirit. Hopes to becoming the pipeline for anointing

"Hallelujah! Praise God who alone are worthy of receiving all honor and glory."

Prayer for our leader Shiela has been going on for a week. It was in asking for a mind of a leader, like Moses, be poured out in leading the tabernacle prayer through the strengthening of the confidence. So that we may experience the Glory. During today's early Morning Prayer session, God placed numerous prayers upon my heart for the 'walk with bible' group members and its leaders.

An eager expectation began to grow as the news about Rev. David Lee was told to be joining our group today. As the tabernacle prayer time closed in, as I was looking at Rev. David, a thought of our leader becoming filled to a full measure crossed my mind. When the hymnal page 201, "My sins have been forgiven" was being praised, my eyes and body began to shed tears. Is this the tears of Joy?

The gate of the tabernacle was so enormous. I began to worry, as if the gate could not open up. While the confessions were being made at the gate, The Lord as life, as king, who suffered and resurrected; the gate began to open up. The Lord came to greet us with many kinds of animals (multitudes that could have filled the Ark of Noah).

As the Lord held my hands, I began to climb up the stairs at the altar of burnt offerings and prayed for the eradication of my ego. I was throwing the ego around, which so often rises back from death. I prayed by screaming in tears, "Lord please, put an end to it!." Then the Leader said "A fire is falling from the Heavens." I looked and saw a white chest coming down, which was added upon my chest. With a closer look, it turned out to be a coffin that was meant for ridding of my ego, worldly passions, thoughts, greed, envy, jealousy and selfishness. I saw these things placed inside a white coffin, which was soon burnt off. Then, it was taken up to the heaven. I saw it being done and assured myself, 'now it is done'.

By standing in front of the wash basin, we asked for the Spirit of repentance. By placing our sins and faults down through repentance, we waited in hope and in a desire of its fulfillment. A large hand came down, who washed our feet and the hands. And when we felt the large hands hugging us, the tip of our hands began to feel like a burning fire.

At the Bread of Presence, a petition, declaration, in thankfulness of the Walk with the Bible group, my small group, church, family etc... was given in order through the prayer. Then, from my right thumb, I began to feel a poking sensation, like that of a needle. During the prayer of tongues at the altar of incense, I was told to pray for the Deacon Kim Do Hyun. Guessing that the prayer at the bread of presence wasn't sufficient, the prayer was lifted in tongues, which was in unison with the Lord's Spirit. Then, the visions opened up. We were in a tug of war against the Satan, Deacon Kim Do Hyun was in the middle of the rope. In a moment, the rope was on the one side and in the other moment, on the other side. Deacon Kim Do Hyun's face was in an agony. Then, all of a sudden, Deacon Kim Do Hyun's body began to merge with the Lord, in creating a plastic like a barrier around his body. The rope began to descend to our side and we screamed in a victory, giving glory unto the Lord. Hallelujah!

As the vision ended, the Leader was praising in tongues. The Lord told me to note down a spiritual writing. While listening to the praise of tongues, the writing was approaching a one page mark. Today's praise felt more beautiful than the other days like that of Holier sounds in the Heaven. I felt the praise rise up into the Heavens. During it's listening period, my finger pointed to the first noted writings. With persistence, I asked for its meaning, "I am with you." I began to ponder as no answers were given after the writing of 2nd sentence. The leader was beginning to enter into the most holy place.

The blood of Jesus turned into a light at the atonement cover. It, then entered into my body. It would have felt uneasy, if a blood of an individual was put on me. But the blood of the Lord was so Holy and beautiful ... By following the leader into the Ark of the Covenant, I could see the stone tablets, staff and manna that were placed within the Ark. Accompanied by a joyful love, all the relics were placed in my possession. Today the love of the Lord was made mine, in blossoming its' flowers through the Leader. The Leader encouraged us to go and visit the unbelievers and even to hug them with this love, in turning the world white with joy. Without a doubt, the Love of our Lord is the best influence. With this love, even the dead will rise.

"But you are a chosen people, a royal priesthood, a holy nation, a people belonging to God, that you may declare the praises of him who called you out of darkness into his wonderful light" (1 Peter 2:9)

The leader disappeared after having dance around on a green pasture across the river. And I arrived at a valley by flying with the Lord. It was such a pure place. The Lord spoke.

"Drink this water. This water is the water stated in Galatians 2:20."

Taking it by faith, after having drunk the water, I shared the joy of it with the Lord. Also, even after the over flowing anointing at the bread of presence had ended, my mind continued to be joyful. I want to become the pipeline of the Lords anointing, to share with everyone who is reading this. Hallelujah!

Moving in Spirit across the time

My father passed away 5 months ago. The high blood pressure that started 2 years ago caused the fall during his way to a restroom, during his wife's absence. He passed away within a day and a half. After having received a call from my sister, I rushed over to Korea with my second child.

With God's providence, my elder child Ji-Woo was on a short term mission trip to Cambodia and was back in Korea for the ministry for disabled. On the last day of the mission trip, the news of the deceased grandfather reached us.

Three days before this incident, my prayer of tongue was unceasing and even on the day of hearing this news, I had stayed up all night praying in tongues. My father had received a baptism three years ago, but had barely lived out the life of faith. Being so worried, every thought was placed into a prayer of repentance in regard to my father's sins. After having repented over and over beside the bed of my unconscious father, I explained regarding Jesus to my father in Spirit. It was the most desperate prayer in my life time.

All of a sudden, the prayer came to an abrupt stop. I began to think that it was my father's spirit having departed. Then, I saw an image of my father smiling. I cried so much ... If God would have extended his life, I could have held his hand one more time, this longing began to settle in, accompanied by a peaceful mind that the Lord was giving. I was able to descend from the plane with a foreknowledge of his passing.

Already having passed the five month mark of the tabernacle prayer, today's prayer was unusually full of internet interference. With a lack of focus at the starting stage of the tabernacle prayer, I could begin to measure up the results of a prayer from previous training. At times, focus would be disrupted but by regaining the focus, grace began to pour out continually.

'Jesus as life', began to wrap around my forehead as a green bandana. 'Jesus as King', began to wrap around my face as a purple bandana. 'Jesus having suffered' became a red linen around my chest. 'Jesus as the resurrection' became a white linen surrounding my stomach. As the gate of the tabernacle began to open, I climbed unto the altar of burnt offerings and offered myself. "Lord, I thank you that you have accepted me as a holy offering." After having repented at the wash basin, we arrived at the bread of presence. But the interference of connectivity was so bad that it was hard to hear. Regardless, I began to refocus and with a fervent heart, began to speak "Amen" in response to the Leader's prayer. Having invited the Holy Spirit, a petition of light, in seeking out my inner most darkness was lifted up. Then, proceeded to pray in tongues at the altar of incense.

The interference went on, but my lips were praising in tongues without any recollection. Without words, with a simple humming, I was already with the Lord at my mother's house in Kyung Ki Do Korea. My mother, who had lost her husband just a couple months ago, was asleep. The Lord reached out his hand in caressing my mother's face that was deepened with pain, began to speak "I am right beside you."

Next, we went onto my brother's house. The Lord began to cry with his gaze fixed on my brother. "I am waiting on you." I cried with him. He was married to an unbelieving woman with a vast wealth. This son's burden of an unbelieving rock like substance was being crushed under the weight of a heavy hammer. Then, the Lord began to lay his hands on my younger sister and cousins, repeating the words of "I love you."

Then, we visited the school, where my first daughter was attending. The Lord laid his hands upon my daughter, who was in a class that seemed to be a freeing atmosphere. Ji-Woo turned around for a brief moment, then went back to reading her book. Now, we went to the younger daughter's school. The Lord laid hands on the child, who was busy fiddling on herdesk. Jenny scratched her head. I might have smiled a bit during this course.

Lastly, the Lord took me back to a long past. I looked like a six years old. My mother clothed me with a blue skirt and white stalkings, telling me that we were going on a trip with my father. The place I was holding hands with my father was on a beach. We looked so happy on the dock near the beach. I cried, because we had visited and walked on the beach so many times in my younger days. Then the Lord spoke to me, "I am with your father. Now, let go of those burdens."

Through laughs and tears, I lifted up endless thankfulness. By moving further inside, the leader spoke at the Ark of the Covenant, "Now, a way has been made for us in spirit that surpasses time and place." Hallelujah! Hallelujah! One of the great aspects within the tabernacle prayer is that in one way or another, assurance is made through your group. In entering through the Ark of the Covenant in laughter and cries, a paper made bell (those often seen during the Christmas season) began to come down. When I asked "What is that?," above the origami, a net like presents came down one by one. A large one fell in front of me, which opened, presenting "Encouragement" and "Order". Then the 9 fruits of the Holy Spirit began to open up, "love," "joy," "peace," "kindness," "goodness," "faithfulness," "gentleness," "self-control." All these words encircled around me and began to dance around me. When a thought came across my mind in 'not seeing "patience." Immediately, the Lord carried "patience" to me and implanted it within my heart.

"My lovely daughter, my eyes never leave you. Truly ... a loving daughter of mine." This tabernacle prayer was filled by grace. Though, the interference of internet with a static noise trained my focusing abilities, the Lord added grace. The more I pray the tabernacle prayer, more things begin to come through an understanding view of detail and clarity. The love of the Lord to me becomes more evident and the love that thirsts after his love begins to indwell each moment.

"Hallelujah! Unto the Lord all the glory!"

Rev. David Lee

Blood of the Lord that heals the forgotten wounds

Hymn number 193 opened up the tabernacle prayer session, "Are you cleansed by the blood of the Lord on the cross." I was entering the tabernacle without even trying today. During the course of burning myself up at the Altar of burnt offerings, the death of ego was repeatedly being explained. I kept burning the ego through persistence, which kept staying alive. The water at the wash basin began to turn into a blood. Jesus began pouring out the blood on each members of the team, one by one.

Prayer of Tongues were being lifted up at the Altar of incense. It was then, the heavens began to open up with angels in a descending line. The Angels stood behind each members, then took up our prayers up to the heaven. This was repeated through the ascending and descending.

"The smoke of the incense, together with the prayers of the saints, went up before God from the angel's hand" (Rev 8:4).

The Lord sitting on the throne smiled, as he laid his eyes upon us. We responded to the Lord in praises of tongue. Jesus was within the white clouds, which I was riding on as well. By meditating the cross at the atonement cover, a girl about 12 years old stood with a stiff expression in front of me (As if this was real, the view was very vivid). As I sprinkled the blood of Jesus, the Holy Spirit said that the girl was 'me'. I almost fell back in a surprise, as I sprinkled the blood on the child. If I was not a leading the prayer, this would have resulted a full loss from shedding in tears.

My mother got remarried at my 4th grade elementary. This event was such a shameful and agonizing experience for a young child like me. I kept my mouth shut at home and made the church my hiding place. It was not because I believed Jesus that led me to the church, rather because I wanted a hiding place. When the summer Bible camps began, I spent the night at the church to attend the Bible camp. Because my step father disliked church, I attended church in a secret. Whenever I came back from the church, the house was in an uproar. Regardless, the church was my only way out.

As maturity came, more freedom was given to me. No one stopped me from going to the church anymore. It was within this phase that the love of God was experienced and the love for the things of this world did not make sense. But God had taken my misconception of being in a completely healed state to my younger pains of life and healed them.

Even before the marriage, I prayed an early morning prayer at the church for the salvation of my parent's souls. At times, I would come home with my eyes swollen. My mother had been involved in a cult. But Jesus visited my mother, who is now an awesome prayer warrior and prays for me. Even from a brief phone call conversation, she said that she was praying before the call. Hallelujah! My father received salvation as well and before his passing, he saw visions of angels coming down to take him up.

As I poured out the blood of Jesus, the girl smiled. Even the forgotten pasts were healed through the Lord. The Lord spoke like this: The difficult environment and pains of my younger childhood will become the base of my ministry and that these things will begin to make sense as a necessary training period for me. It is because now I can understand the difficult family situations and the children of the remarried families will be able to hear my story during their struggles. And that is why I prayed a lot for a believing husband, which God in answer gave me an uncooked potato. Anyway, I am walking the path of a pastoral ministry now. Hallelujah! When the atonement cover opened up, with a bright light, endless words written in "Love you," kept rising up. In trying to calm myself down, I began to speak the words from the Holy Spirit.

"Dear lovely Children, Be at peace, be at peace, be at peace. Do not be swayed by the situation. Armies of Angels are working around you. Be victorious, rise up. Fix your eyes upon me and rise."

The angles were protecting us from the attacks of Satan. At the budded staff, he asked for my one hope and said that the hope given in faith would result in reality. Then, I was told to look inside the jar of manna, it contained a pure living water. This was said to be the 'life', and this life would revive the souls. As this water was to be passed out to the unbelieving souls, I passed them out to my sister and my mother.

I felt at ease, as the clouds from the sky entered through my body. The Lord came out to meet us. I held unto the Lord's hand and walked out to the sports field. The Lord asked me to run a relay. And because there was no way to hold my laughter, by pressing the mute button, I laughed out as much as possible. Perhaps the Lord has done this surprising event as an encouragement in response to the shedding of tears. Not only has the Lord cleansed me with the Blood, but also healed my forgotten past pains.

"Lord, thank you. I had forgotten, but now it is completely cleansed. I Live to the Lord and Die to the Lord, I am yours. I will live my life as a messenger of the Cross. Lord, I love you so much. Hallelujah!"

God, who works through the Tabernacle Prayer

Through the 5th tabernacle prayer, I am strengthened by prophesies. Previously, this wouldn't haven't been so. For example, a person being lifted up during a prayer, at times are revealed of their spiritual state in accordance to the needs of an individual. One time, I saw my back view as I walked along side by side with Jesus. At first, it looked as if Jesus had placed his hands on my back during the walk. But with a closer observation, there could be seen a fire coming out from the hand of Jesus!

"Lord, what is this?"

"I am healing your back."

This was not only for me but for everyone in the tabernacle prayer session, healing fire was being spread out to everyone. Then, Jesus placed his hands on my right chest.

"and Lord, what does this mean?"

"I am healing the problems of the mind."

In the next Tabernacle Prayer session, the anointing of a healing was poured out. I could sense my hands becoming hot. One of the members mentioned an experience of nearly falling backwards. Later on, I saw the visions regarding that member, that member was laying hands on a child's stomach. An understanding came about, 'Ah! The anointing of healing is being poured out on that member.' But because we were all praying as a group, this could not be prophesied out due to its personal basis.

In the following tabernacle prayer session, by the immense presence of God, each members were proclaiming through the prayer of tongues, of prophesy and words of God.

"Even though you all pray, sometimes it does not make it up to the Heavens but rather descends. Cry out in power. With the power, penetrate through the forces that block your prayers. Do not give up but pray until the end. You are all great warriors. My beautiful bride. Can you give birth to the Spiritual children? Also, your talents are covered in a dust. Dig out the talents that are buried. Put them into use."

I cannot recall all the details but an understanding of "God did it all" came about by talking with each members within the group. The visions that I saw regarding the member who was laying hands on a child said that the member's child was sick that day. Due to the situational circumstances, the vision of that member could not be disclosed that day but about 2 days later (after the tabernacle prayer session), a chance was given to talk to that member one on one. So I told the member to lay hands on the child's stomach and pray. It was clear that God was wanting to heal the child through the visions. Also, the words of an encouragement and spiritual things that God had poured out on me regarding that member was shared. An assurance speaks for a further sharing in the future. Through the tabernacle prayer, the spiritual fear of that member was disclosed. Then, the intercessory prayers in relation to that member given brought about an understanding. That is why praying together is powerful and effective in experiencing God in our daily lives.

Every single member in our group feels close like a family member. I feel the warm love through the encouragements, praying and wishing the best for each other. Through books, we encourage each other. When the Bible verses were sent out to each other, the will of God was understood in each member's lives as a remedy, which resulted in three different physical healing. Especially, a member named Marry Hill's difficulty in obtaining an Indian visa for 6 month was solved through a consular, who in turn allowed a one year visa. We were all so thankful. Whenever there was a problem, we would send texts in request of prayers. Whenever a good news was brought about, the members were so eager to share it with the tabernacle prayer leader. How precious and beautiful are my members. How much more so would God delight in them!

"Lord. Bless the members. I love you. I thank you. Hallelujah! Lord, unto you all the Glory."

About the Author

Pastor David Lee came to America Twenty years ago.

Having performed and studied as an opera singer in America for Ten years, a calling was found in his life as a Pastor.

He was commissioned through the Korean American Presbyterian Church and began a Church.

After having heard the Voice of God, Pastor David began to understand the secret of the Tabernacle Prayer.

He established (www.WalkingWithBible.com) and is spreading the Tabernacle Prayer. Jesus's references of praying in Secret is a recreation of the Tabernacle Prayer.

This prayer will establish a deeper presence of God's Glory, healing of the sick and manifestation of God's Glory.

Pastor David was fully supported at the University of Arizona in Bachelors and University of Hartford in Masters.

Then, enrolled at one of the prestigious schools, Gordon-Conwell Theological Seminary for the Pastoral Study.

Contact: www.TabernaclePrayer.org
(770-335-6628)
Rev. Lee

Printed in the United States
By Bookmasters